Aviation Elite Units

No 60 Sqn
RFC/RAF

Aviation Elite Units • 41

No 60 Sqn
RFC/RAF

Alex Revell
Series editor Tony Holmes

Front Cover
On the morning of 19 May 1917, the pilots of C Flight No 60 Sqn RFC were sitting in their Nieuport scouts about to take off on patrol when a German Albatros suddenly appeared out of the layer of low cloud and flew across the aerodrome at 1,000ft. Seeing the British scouts, the German pilot, realising his mistake, quickly flew back into the cloud cover. On the ground, amid great excitement and confusion, pilots were hurriedly taking off in pursuit. William Fry was first in the air and coming through the clouds he saw the Albatros just ahead. 'I gave chase, firing a few bursts but was too excited at first to take proper aim through the sight.' The enemy pilot, deciding that discretion was the better part of valour, hurriedly landed, turning the Albatros over onto its back. A delighted 'Willie' Fry – 'it was the ambition of every young pilot to bring down a German on our side of the lines' – landed close by and shook hands with his captive, who admitted that he was lost. Taken back to the unit's mess for lunch the enemy pilot was plied with strong drink and questioned. He steadfastly refused to give any information other than his rank and name, Ltn Georg Noth, but admitted that he was a member of the famed *Jasta* Boelcke. The stub of a ticket for the previous evening's performance at a theatre in Cambrai was found in the pocket of his tunic. One evening a carefree theatre-goer, the next day a prisoner. Such are the fortunes of war (*Cover artwork by Mark Postlethwaite*)

First published in Great Britain in 2011 by Osprey Publishing, Midland House, West Way, Botley, Oxford OX2 0PH, UK
44-20 23rd St, Suite 219, Long Island City, NY 11101, USA

E-mail; info@ospreypublishing.com

Osprey Publishing is part of the Osprey Group

A CIP catalogue record for this book is available from the British Library

ISBN: 978 1 84908 333 1
E-book ISBN: 978 1 84908 334 8

Page design by Mark Holt
Cover Artwork by Mark Postlethwaite
Aircraft Profiles by Harry Dempsey
Index by Alan Thatcher
Originated by United Graphics Pte Ltd
Printed and bound in China through Bookbuilders

11 12 13 14 15   10 9 8 7 6 5 4 3 2 1

Osprey Publishing is supporting the Woodland Trust, the UK's leading woodland conservation charity by funding the dedication of trees.

www.ospreypublishing.com

ACKNOWLEDGEMENTS
My thanks to my fellow researchers worldwide, who as always have given unstinted help. My special thanks to all those who supplied documents and many invaluable photographs: Mike O'Connor, Norman Franks, Russ Gannon, Colin Huston, Jeff Jefford, Bernard Klaeylé, Les Rogers, and Greg VanWyngarden. My special thanks, as always, to Harry Dempsey for both the care and excellence of his artwork. My thanks also to Charly and Kate for their invaluable help and understanding.

CONTENTS

A TROUBLED START

On 3 August 1916, Major General Trenchard, Commanding Officer of the Royal Flying Corps, wrote to Field Marshal Haig, Commander in Chief of the British Army in France, 'I have had to withdraw one of the GHQ fighting squadrons from work temporarily, and have sent it to St-André-au Bois. This squadron, since the battle began, has lost a squadron commander, two flight commanders and one pilot, all killed and missing and yesterday it lost two more machines with two pilots and observers to anti-aircraft fire. Besides this they have had several officers wounded. They have a difficult machine to fly, and I think a rest away from work is absolutely essential.'

It was an inauspicious beginning for a squadron which was to become one of the most successful fighter squadrons of the RFC and RAF.

FORMATION

No 60 Sqn was formed at Gosport on 15 May 1916 under the command of Major Francis Waldron – universally known throughout the RFC as 'Ferdy' – from No 1 Aeroplane Reserve Squadron. Unlike other squadrons, which received their aeroplanes in England, then flew them to France, the unit was to be equipped with French Morane-Saulnier types on its arrival in France. On 26 May, only four of the unit's training aeroplanes at Gosport, two Morane-Saulnier Type LA Parasol monoplanes, and two BB Type Biplanes, were flown to France. The Parasols were flown by Lt C F Portal and 2Lt C A Ridley;

A Morane-Saulnier Type LA. These Moranes had a maximum speed of 88 mph at 6500 ft and an endurance of 2½ hours. Four Type LA were issued to No 60 Sqn in France, but by the end of June 1916 the unit had none on charge. At the beginning of August one machine (A143) was issued for the landing of spies in German held territory and was lost on 3 August

A Morane-Saulnier Type BB 5167. These Moranes were powered by a 110 hp Le Rhône engine, and had a maximum speed of 83 mph at 10,000 ft, with a service ceiling of 12,000 ft. They were armed with two 0.303 Lewis machine guns: one on the upper wing, fired by the pilot, but reloaded by the observer, and a rear mounted Lewis gun for the observer. No 60 Sqn operated 15 of the type during 1916, the last being returned to No 1 Aeroplane Supply Depot (1ASD) on 29 January 1917. 5167 was written off in a crash on 23 June 1916

Maj F F Waldron (left) and Capt R R Smith-Barry. After Waldron was killed in action on 3 July 1916, Smith-Barry took command of No 60 Sqn

Capt D'Urban Victor Armstrong. A South African, Armstrong claimed only one victory while serving with the unit, but was awarded another four in 1918 while flying as a night fighter pilot in No 151 Sqn. He was known throughout the RFC for his skill as an aerobatic pilot, particularly with the notoriously difficult Sopwith Camel, but was killed when stunting in one on 13 November 1918 (*M O'Connor*)

A Morane Type N. These Moranes, known as Bullets, were powered with an 80 hp Le Rhône 9C engine. Maximum speed was 89 mph at sea level with an endurance of 1hr 20mins. Armament was a 0.303 Lewis machine gun. No 60 Sqn was issued with 22 of these machines, which were replaced by Type I and Type V Bullets. These latter types, of similar configuration, were powered with an 110 hp Le Rhône 9J engine and were extremely unpopular with the unit's pilots. Lt W M Fry, who flew in the RFC and RAF during the first war, the inter-war years and World War 2, and during his long career flew many types of aircraft, confided to the author that the 110 hp Morane Bullet was the only aeroplane he felt was actively trying to kill him

Lt H H Balfour. Harold Balfour learnt to fly at his own expense, but served in France with his regiment, the King's Royal Rifle Company, for three months before his request for a transfer to the RFC was approved. After serving with No 60 Sqn for two months he was transferred to Martlesham Heath as a test pilot. He later returned to France as Flight commander in 43 Sqn, flying Sopwith 1½ Strutters, where he scored nine victories and was awarded a Military Cross (MC). Retiring from the RAF in 1926 he became a politician and was Under Secretary of State for Air in 1938. As Lord Balfour of Inche he was an active member both of the House of Lords and President of Cross and Cockade International (*The First World War Aviation Historical Society GB*)

the BB Biplanes by 2Lt A Bell-Irving and one other pilot, possibly 2Lt H Meintjes. Two days later the remainder of the squadron personnel crossed to France by boat and took up its quarters at St Omer, moving to nearby Boisdinghem three days later. While at Boisdinghem the unit received its aeroplanes: A Flight was equipped with four Morane Type N monoplanes, known to the RFC as the Morane Bullet, B Flight was allocated four Parasols and C Flight four Type BB Biplanes. The Parasols were used for training purposes only and before the squadron moved to its first operational base at Vert Galant on 16 June 1916 they were replaced by additional Bullets, allocated to C Flight. More pilots were posted in and as the date of its first operations approached the unit consisted of A and C Flight equipped with Morane Bullets, with B Flight retaining the BB Type Biplanes.

At Vert Galant No 60 Sqn came under the orders of 9th Wing, the Wing's three squadrons – Nos 21, and 27, plus an element of No 70 Sqn, and now No 60 Sqn – providing a tactical reserve which could be moved to any part of the British front as or when it was required. It was now the middle of June and the build up of the British forces for the coming battle of the Somme had begun.

No 60 Sqn flew its first patrols on the afternoon of 17 June. Patrols of two Bullets, alternating with two Biplanes, covered the area between Arras and Albert. These initial patrols highlighted the difficulties of operating aeroplanes of mixed types – the Biplanes were faster than the Bullets – and patrols flown by A and C Flights were increased to Flight strength, with B Flight operating its Biplanes. Another difficulty was the similarity of the Bullets to the German Fokker E.III.

Flying a patrol on 26 June, the Bullets were fired on by British anti-aircraft guns; it was evident that some form of recognition aid was needed. After some experiments, the spinners and cowlings of the Bullets were painted red, which was later extended on the fuselage to include the undercarriage and cabane. Photographic evidence shows that a red line was also painted on a fuselage longeron of the Bullets and Biplanes, extending to the rudder.

THE SOMME

The battle of the Somme opened on the morning of 1 July. No 60 Sqn had four Morane Biplanes and nine Morane Bullets on strength. In addition to escorting bombing raids by the RE 7s and BE 2cs of No 21 Sqn and the Martinsydes of No 27 Sqn, the Bullets flew offensive patrols (OPs) on the first day of the battle. In one of these Maj Waldron scored the unit's first victory, forcing an enemy LVG to land near Bapaume just after 1145hrs. The next day, Lts C Patteson and W E G Bryant, in a Biplane, drove a Fokker E.III down out of control and another Biplane crew claimed a second Fokker forced to land, both over the German side.

On the morning of 3 July, 'Ferdy' Waldron led five Bullets in a patrol to decoy attention away from BE 2cs attacking St Quentin. Lts J H Simpson and D V Armstrong fell out with engine trouble, but Waldron, Lt H H Balfour and Capt R R Smith-Barry flew on, above the Arras to Cambrai road. Approaching Cambrai, a formation of enemy two-seaters, led by a Fokker E Type was seen, followed by two additional Fokker monoplanes, bringing the number of enemy machines to around a dozen. Undeterred by these odds, Waldron immediately led Balfour and Smith-Barry in an attack. Harold Balfour later wrote: 'I'm sure they were not contemplating war at all but Ferdy pointed us towards them and led us straight in. My next impressions were rather mixed. I seemed to be surrounded by Huns in two-seaters'. Waldron was outmanoeuvred and attacked by a two-seater, flown by Uffz Howe of *FA 5b*. Balfour saw that his CO was in trouble and succeeded in driving off the enemy, but the damage was done. Waldron had been badly wounded, and although he managed to crash land his damaged Morane behind the enemy lines, he died of his wounds that night.

After Waldron's death on 3 July 1916, his Morane Bullet A175 was crudely reconstructed by the Germans

Morane Type N A128. Capt N A Browning-Paterson was killed in action flying this Bullet on 21 July 1916

The loss of its CO was a blow to No 60 Sqn. Waldron had flown at least one patrol a day as an example to his pilots and was a pilot of great experience, experience which the RFC needed at this time of expansion, and his loss brought an order from RFC HQ that squadron commanders would no longer fly over the lines. Robert Smith-Barry was given command of the squadron.

There were no further combat claims until 11 July, when Capt H C Tower and Lt Henry Meintjes each claimed a Fokker over the Bois de Havrincourt. The two Bullets were escorting a bombing raid led by a BE 2c piloted by Lt Col Hugh Dowding, the CO of 9th Wing, with Capt Longridge as his gunner. Six RE 7s of No 21 Sqn and ten Martinsydes of No 27 Sqn were escorted by additional Martinsydes and the Bullets of No 60 Sqn. The British formation was attacked by six enemy machines over the Bois de Havrincourt and both Dowding and Longridge were slightly wounded before Tower and Meintjes drove off the attackers.

Although Nos 21 and 27 Sqns were in action over the next ten days, no escorts were flown by No 60 Sqn, but on 21 July Capt A S M Summers and Lt L E Whitehead took off in BB Biplanes armed with Le Prieur rockets to attack enemy balloons. These attacks were unsuccessful and in an evening patrol Captain Norman Browning-Paterson was shot down in flames by Ltn Wintgens of *KEK Vaux* for his tenth victory of an eventual nineteen.

The loss of Browning-Paterson was the beginning of a run of casualties. In an evening patrol on 26 July Lt L E Whitehead and 2AM E R Deal were attacked by LVGs over Bethune. Deal was shot through the foot and Whitehead landed the badly damaged BB Biplane (A149) at Verquin. Deal was taken to hospital and the Biplane was struck off strength.

The unit was next in action in the early evening of 27 July. A patrol of six Bullets attacked seven LVG two seaters. The enemy pilots had seen the Bullets but had mistaken them for Fokkers; in their turn the British pilots had first thought the enemy machines were friendly Martinsydes. It was not until the two formations were within 200 yards of each other that 2Lt S F Vincent realised that the two-seaters were 'covered in black crosses, not roundels'. The Flight Commander, Capt J Simpson, fired a red Very light, the signal to attack, but in doing so he lost control of his Bullet, which stalled and went into a spin.

Stanley Vincent selected an enemy machine: 'we circled decorously around each other in a left-hand circuit'. Vincent had difficulty tightening the circle in order to bring his Lewis gun to bear, but the enemy gunner was making good shooting at the little Bullet, hitting one of the cabane cables and the windscreen. Vincent took evasive action – 'a split-arse turn'. When he came out of the turn he found the enemy was in front of him, 'under fifty yards away'. Vincent fired only 17 rounds from his Lewis gun before he had a stoppage due to a bulged round, but he saw the enemy pilot throw up one arm before his aeroplane dived away. Having cleared his jam, Vincent found that he was alone in the sky, but was soon joined by Simpson and another Bullet. Landing at Vert Galant, Simpson congratulated Vincent on his victory. Recovered from his spin and climbing back into the fight, the LVG had gone past him and he had seen it crash, 15 miles behind the enemy lines. 2Lt B M Wainwright had driven down another LVG, and 2Lt H G Smart had forced another to land in the German lines, but Vincent was the first pilot of the unit to be credited with an enemy aircraft as crashed. The daughter of the farmer who owned Vert Galant farm, presented Vincent with a bunch of flowers to mark his victory: the accompanying note, 'Felicitations au Lieutenant Vincent, ' became one of the squadron's souvenirs.

On 30 July a patrol of four Biplanes were over the St Quentin area when they were attacked by an enemy force of LVG two-seaters. One

The wreckage of Morane Type BB Biplane 5181 in German hands. Sgt A Walker and 2Lt L L Clark were both killed (*L Rogers*)

Morane Type Biplane 5177, shot down on 2 August 1916. The pilot, Lt J A N Ormsby, survived the crash, but died of his wounds three days later. The observer, 2Lt H J Newton, was killed

2Lt Claude Ridley. On 3 August 1916, after landing in enemy territory due to engine failure, Ridley evaded capture and returned to England in October. This photograph was taken to obtain a faked passport

Biplane, crewed by Capt L S Charles and Lt C Williams was forced to land. Williams had been killed in the fight, and although Charles was wounded and taken POW, he later died of his wounds. Lt Lewis E Whitehead managed to land his badly damaged Biplane at Baizieux, but he and his observer, 2Lt W Bryant, were both wounded.

This run of casualties continued. On 2 August, German anti-aircraft fire – popularly known as 'Archie' – brought down two Biplanes. Sgt A Walker and his observer, 2Lt L Clark in 5181 were both killed. Flying Biplane 5177, Lt J A N Ormsby survived, but his observer, 2Lt H J Newton, was killed. Ormsby died of his wounds three days later. Both these Biplanes were also claimed as victories by Kurt Wintgens and Wilhelm Frankl of *KEK Vaux*.

SPIES AND ESCAPES

On 29 July, two Morane Parasols had been allocated to the unit for the purpose of landing spies behind the German lines. During practice reconnaissance flights these aircraft were found to be prone to engine failure and on 3 August, 2Lt Claude Ridley, flying Parasol A143 was lost while flying a spy dropping mission. Developing engine trouble near Douai, Ridley was forced to land near Villers en Couchies, overturning the Parasol in a cornfield. Ridley set fire to the Parasol and he and his companion, evading German patrols, made for the Belgian frontier. After many adventures, including Ridley having his head bandaged, posing as a deaf mute and travelling on a forged passport, they finally reached the Dutch border on 10 October and scaled the electrified fence by using a ladder. Back in England, Ridley was able to give valuable information regarding enemy ammunition dumps and aerodromes which he had seen in his travels, almost certainly more information than the original spy could have given. Stanley Vincent later recalled that when forced to land, Ridley, as Mess secretary, had the cash from all their Mess bills in his pocket. However, on learning how useful it had been in bribes during the escape, all was forgiven. Ridley was not allowed to return to France, but was awarded a DSO.

In a month of operations, No 60 Sqn had suffered 12 casualties. Smith-Barry was appalled. He was convinced that many were the result of the inadequate training of his replacement pilots. He informed Dowding, commanding 9th Wing, that he would not send new pilots over the lines with less than seven total hours flying time. Dowding agreed and informed Trenchard, who telegraphed Haig of his decision to withdraw the squadron from active duty.

WITHDRAWN

On 3 August No 60 Sqn was relocated to St. André-au Bois, an aerodrome west of Hesdin on the road to Montreuil, and commenced a period of intense training. On 8 August, King George V visited the chateau at St André, which now housed both GHQ and RFC HQ, and Biplanes and Bullets of the unit flew defensive patrols over the area. On 12 August, the last remaining Biplanes of B Flight were returned to the depot, the Flight re-equipped with 80 hp Bullets, and its observers posted to squadrons operating two-seater aeroplanes.

Of equal importance in Trenchard's decision to rest the unit was the quality of its equipment. B Flight's Morane BB Biplanes were outclassed, even by the almost obsolete Fokker *eindekkers*, and although A Flight continued to fly the 80 hp Morane Type N Bullet, on 29 July C Flight had begun to be re-equipped with the 110 hp Le Rhône-powered Bullet, Type I and V. If the Morane N had been unpopular with the unit's pilots, the new type was universally feared and detested by all. The idea to re-engine the 80 hp Bullet with a 110 hp engine is reputed

Claude Ridley in 1917. Now a Captain, he is wearing an MC for anti-Zeppelin work in 1916 and a DSO awarded for his evasion of capture in 1916.

This Morane Type BB Biplane 5182 was issued to the unit in May 1916, but written off in a crash on 2 August

Like all Morane Bullets, the Type V was notoriously difficult to land. 'Duke' Meintjes stands by A199 after a landing put the Morane up on its nose. Of interest is the unusual position of the Vickers gun, mounted on the port longeron

to have been Trenchard's, who thought that re-engined and re-armed with an interrupted Vickers gun firing through the propeller arc the Bullet would be 'the best machine in the air'. The French manufacturers agreed to build the new type, but only on condition that it should be test flown by the RFC, as they would not allow their own test pilots to fly them. Lt William Mays Fry, who joined the unit on 1 October, recalled in his autobiography, *Air of Battle*, his first flight in one of the 110 hp Bullets. 'I was numbed and almost speechless with fear at having to take the machine into the air, but I wasn't going to show it. The flight sergeant rigger and sergeant fitter gave me all the information they could about the controls and engine, mostly incomprehensible to me, and I ran up the engine and took off.' The Morane had a balanced elevator, with wing warping control for banking, both worked from the control column. This made the machine very light on fore and aft control, but stiff and heavy laterally. Warping the wings to bank was by 'brute force', whereas the balanced elevator control was very light, making it easy, in Fry's recollection, 'to pull the stick right back till the tailplane was nearly at right angles to the line of flight and thus break the flimsy tail off.'

REORGANISATION

In February 1916, the German air force had found that its fighter aeroplanes attached to the *Feldflieger Abteilungen* in two and threes, in similar fashion to the fighters attached to the two-seater squadrons of the RFC, were more effective when grouped together in dedicated fighter units. In late April, Trenchard, profiting from this lesson, decided to concentrate into the Army Wings those single-seater fighters still attached to the two-seater squadrons. The pilots who flew the single-seaters – mainly voluntarily – were individuals suited by both temperament and ability to become fighter pilots: a tight knit hierarchy within the RFC, a small, elite band, mostly known to each other. As a result of this reorganisation, the single-seater Nieuports and their pilots, of Nos 1, 3 and 11 Sqns – squadrons flying mainly two-seater aeroplanes – were posted into No 60 Sqn. On 16 August Lts Douglas Latta MC, Tony Walters and Sidney Parker flew in from No 1 Sqn, and Frank Goodrich, an American serving in No 3 Sqn, was transferred, promoted to captain, and given command of 'A' Flight. Over the next few days, six additional pilots, the entire scout Flight of No 11 Sqn, would arrive at St André, flying in three Type 16 and three Type 17 Nieuports.

A FRESH START

On 23 August, its three weeks of training completed, the unit flew to its new base at Izel-le-Hameau, coming under the orders of 13 (Army) Wing, 3rd Brigade. On the same day, Lt Albert Ball flew into Izel to

Officers' huts at Izel-le-Hameau (*L Rogers*)

Capt Albert Ball standing in front of his Nieuport. Born in Nottingham in August 1896, Ball learnt to fly at Hendon while serving with the Sherwood Foresters and transferred to the RFC in October 1915. After flying in France with Nos 13,11 and 8 Sqns, he was posted to 60 Sqn on 23 August 1916. At the time of his posting, Ball had been awarded 11 victories and was the RFC's highest scoring fighter pilot. Ball served with No 60 Sqn until 3 October, adding another 20 victories and winning an MC and a DSO and Bar

Lt J M Drysdale here pictured in civilian clothes. (*M O'Connor*)

join the unit from No 11 Sqn, bringing his Nieuport (A201). At this time Ball was the RFC's foremost fighter pilot with 11 victories.

The squadron now operated two Flights of Nieuports and one of Morane Bullets and its first combat reports to 13th Wing showed that the period of training was bearing fruit. On 24 August Capt H C Tower drove down an enemy machine over Adinfer Wood and the following day, two days after his arrival, Ball shot down a Roland C II out of control south of Arras. On the debit side, Lt J M Drysdale was wounded by 'Archie' and taken to hospital.

Those pilots still flying the Bullets also gained victories. On 27 August, 2Lt H G Smart drove down a Roland over Bapaume at 0935 hrs and at 1100 hrs 2Lt B M Wainwright sent another down out of control south of Arras.

Ball added to his score with a treble on 28 August when he shot down two Rolands and a 'C' Type during the day. The first Roland,

Morane Type N A173 after capture on 28 August 1916. The pilot, 2Lt B W Wainwright, was taken prisoner

which was from *Fl Abt* 207, was shot down just after 0700 hrs. Ball's fire killed the pilot, Ltn Joachim von Arnim, but the observer, Ltn Böhne managed to land the damaged machine near Transloy. In the evening, flying an escort duty, Ball attacked four hostile machines flying south-east of Adinfer, shooting down the nearest, a Roland, which crashed just east of Ayette. Ball then forced another Roland to land north of Grevillers.

Capt A D Bell-Irving had also been successful during the evening. Flying a Bullet (A166) he destroyed a Roland C II over Bapaume at 1840 hrs and Tony Walters in a Nieuport (A164) sent an LVG down out of control 20 minutes later.

Three Bullets flew an escort for the BEs of No 8 Sqn during the evening. Six LVGs climbed to attack the bombers and Melvyn Wainwright dived out of the sun to attack the rear two. He drove one off, but he was now a long way east of the lines. Mindful of the prevailing westerly wind, he turned for home, but was attacked by two of the LVGs, the fire from one hitting his windscreen and engine, which stopped. Wainwright force landed and was taken prisoner.

Maj Smith-Barry asked Ball to submit a list of his victory claims and combats: these amounted to 84 combats; 11 machines and one balloon brought down and seen to crash; 12 machines forced down and damaged, plus a further five machines forced down but not seen to crash. This total made Ball the leading British pilot, with 15 officially confirmed victories over aeroplanes, plus a balloon, although Ball himself wrote home that he thought it to be only 12 machines crashed and the balloon. By the end of August Ball's official score stood at 17.

There was a great deal of fighting on the last day of the month. In the morning, at 1000 hrs, 2Lt P S Joyce was fighting a black Fokker E Type over Bapaume when he was attacked by an enemy biplane. Capt Alfred Summers saw this and attacked the enemy machine, forcing it to dive away. At 1145 hrs, Capt Frank Goodrich, in Nieuport A200, leading another Nieuport and two Bullets, attacked four enemy machines over

Nieuport 16 A135, fitted with Le Prieur rockets. Issued to the unit in August 1916, it was flown by James Latta, who scored two victories flying this machine

Transloy. Goodrich fired a drum and a half into one of the enemy machines, an LVG, which went down out of control through the clouds at 3000 ft. Douglas Latta flew two patrols in the evening. He had no success in the first, but in his second he attacked eight LVGs and sent one down out of control over Bapaume.

Ball took off alone in the evening. He flew to an enemy aerodrome near Cambrai and watched 12 Rolands taking off. Ball attacked these, crashing one and forcing another to land. During these attacks the ignition system of his Nieuport was hit and he glided over the lines and landed at Colincamp, spending the night with his Nieuport. These successes brought Ball's score to 20 official victories and he was awarded a DSO and Bar to add to the Military Cross (MC) he had won in July.

On 1 September, the unit moved a few miles north-west to Savy, sharing the aerodrome with No 13 Sqn. The personnel were billeted in the Marie and the farm buildings, but Ball was able to return to the hut he had built while stationed there with No 11 Sqn, settling in before he left on ten days' leave.

For the first week of the month, bad weather of low cloud and mist curtailed flying and the opportunity was taken to ferry B Flight's remaining Bullets to the depot at Candas, replacing them with Nieuports. On 12 September the unit lost one of its most popular members in a tragic accident. Both Capt Frank Goodrich and Lt Sidney Parker had come to the end of their tours of duty and were returning to England. A farewell party was planned: Parker left to buy champagne in St Pol and Goodrich, the A Flight commander,

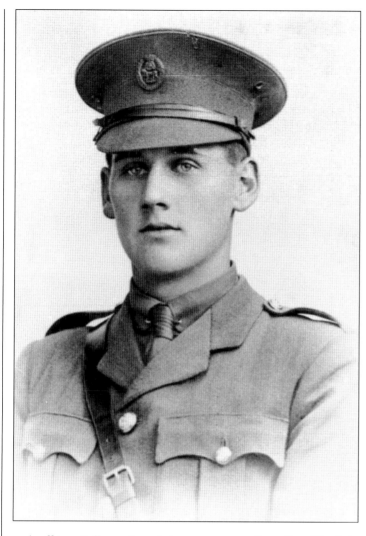

Lt S E Parker. A Canadian, Sidney
Parker was posted to the unit from
No 1 Sqn on 16 August 1916,
returning to England on 12
September. He was later posted to
Gosport as an instructor and
became a member of Smith-Barry's
School of Special Flying
(*M O'Connor*)

Capt A S M Summers was killed
in action on 15 September 1916
(*M O'Connor*)

took off in a Bullet to fly to Lahoussoye, to say farewell to friends in
his old squadron, No 3. After take-off the popular American put
the Bullet into a steep climb, but it stalled and Goodrich was killed
in the crash.

The third and final phase of the battle of the Somme opened on
15 September with the British 4th Army attacking between Morval and
Le Sars. Orders from Wing had specified that German observation
balloons were to be attacked on the day before the opening of the
offensive and Alan D Bell-Irving and Ball attacked two balloons
at Avesnes-le-Bapaume with Le Prieur rockets, Bell-Irving setting one
balloon alight. On the morning of the offensive three enemy balloons
were in positions to overlook British tanks taking part, and Trenchard
visited the unit, asking for volunteers to destroy them. Capts Ball,
Summers and 2Lts Tony Walters and E J L W Gilchrist, all took off
in Nieuports armed with Le Prieur rockets. Euan Gilchrist destroyed
his balloon and although Alfred Summers was credited with destroying
another, he was shot down in flames by the defending anti-aircraft
batteries.

Ball and Walters found that their balloons had been taken down, so they attacked a formation of LVGs and Fokker D Types to the north-east of Bapaume. Ball fired all eight of his rockets at one of the Fokkers from a range of 200 yards, but missed. He then closed to 50 yards and fired half a drum of Lewis. The Fokker went down to crash just east of Beugny. Walters had better luck with his rockets, hitting one of the LVGs in the fuselage and setting it alight, the burning machine finally crashing near Bapaume.

In their attacks on the balloons, the Nieuports were escorted by Bullets. Lts R M Hill and C W Carlyle shared in the destruction of a Roland C Type over Bapaume and 2Lt Edwin S T Cole sent another down out of control. In an afternoon patrol, Ball attacked

Capt Ernest Leslie Foot. One of the early, skilful, and most respected pilots of the RFC, Foot was awarded three victories while in No 11 Sqn. He added another two with No 60 Sqn before he was shot down in flames on 26 October 1916. Foot was unhurt in the crash but was returned to Home Establishment (HE) on 3 November. He was killed in 1923 in a flying accident

a two-seater from *Fl Abt* 221. His fire wounded the observer, Ltn von Wurmb in the arm, but the enemy pilot landed his machine near Nurlu. In the evening, at 1900 hrs, Ball destroyed a Roland C.II. from *Jasta 13*, the enemy machine crashing north-east of Bertincourt. The pilot, Uffz H Carstens and his observer, Oblt E Cornu, were both wounded, Cornu dying of his wounds two days later. To replace the loss of Summers, the B Flight Commander, Capt Ernest Leslie Foot was posted in, bringing with him a Spad 7 (A253) for operational trials.

Although the weather improved on 18 September there was little flying, but in the early evening of the following day a reconnaissance by FE 2bs of No 11 Squadron, escorted by a mixed formation of Morane Bullets and Nieuports from No 60 Sqn, were attacked by 20 enemy fighters over Bapaume. Some of the enemy machines were from *Jasta* 2 and Hptm Oswald Boelcke, the Staffelführer, shot down Capt H C 'Jimmy' Tower in flames. Boelcke related: 'Six of us rattled into a squadron consisting of eight or ten FEs and several Moranes – the fat lattice tails down below and the Moranes above as cover. I engaged one of the latter and pranced about the air with him – he escaped me for a moment, but I got to grips with him again west of Bapaume; one of my guns jammed but the other shot all the better. I shot up that monoplane from close range until he broke up in flames and fell into the wood near Grévillers in fragments.'

Under the aggressive attacks by the German fighters, the reconnaissance was abandoned. Three of the FEs were badly shot up. One of the Bullets, flown by Lt L S Weedon, was badly damaged by fire from a 'small biplane', which shot away the outer warp control wire on the port side of the Morane and Weedon could make only

Foot's Spad 7, A253, which he brought with him on his posting to the unit for operational trials. Foot scored one victory in A253

turns to starboard. When he landed back at base – luckily, a smooth landing – it was found that his port wing was so badly damaged that it could have broken off at any moment. Two Fokkers were claimed as seen to crash during the fight, one as a result of a collision with a Morane, but there were no reported German casualties. With the loss of Tower, the unit had lost three Flight commanders in a space of ten days. Capt Eustace O Grenfell was posted in as C Flight commander.

In an evening patrol on 21 September, flying Nieuport A213, marked A1 and fitted with a spinner painted bright red, Ball scored another treble. Attacking a formation of Rolands north of Bapaume at 1600 hrs, he first fired his Le Prieur rockets to scatter the enemy machines, then attacked a Roland, firing a full drum. The enemy pilot made a crash landing near a railway line. Ball then engaged a second Roland, firing two full drums into it. The enemy machine crashed at 1605 hrs, close by the first. Ball took off again at 1715 hrs and at 1800 hrs, 7000 ft over Bucquoy, he attacked a pair of Roland C IIs, 3000 ft below him. These made off east, but later returned and Ball attacked them again, sending one down in a flat spin. After driving the remaining Roland east, Ball returned and searched the ground for its companion. The wreckage was lying across a hedge. Ball dived to 500 ft and fired two full drums into the remains of the Roland, 'to make certain of the passengers'. This action was uncharacteristic of Ball and indicative of the state of his nerves. That night he approached Smith-Barry, requesting a rest from operations, giving as a reason that he was taking unnecessary risks, a sure sign that his nerves were bad. Nerves or not, Ball was fighting again the next day, forcing a Roland to land during an escort patrol in the morning and destroying a Fokker D Type east of Bapaume at 1700 hrs. During the day, George Philippi sent an LVG down out of control near Bapaume and 2Lts A M Walters and G O Smart both claimed victories. Smart, flying a Bullet (A202) drove down an LVG over Bapaume at 1100 hrs; 30 minutes later, Walters, flying Nieuport A201, drove down another.

In the morning patrols the next day, only Bell-Irving scored, destroying a Roland C II over Croisilles at 1230 hrs, but in the evening Ball sent an Albatros C Type down in flames over Mory at 1800 hrs. This was possibly a machine from *Fl Abt* 41, crewed by Oblt Minor and Ltn Kliche, both killed. On 25 September, at 1830 hrs, Ball fought an Albatros C Type from *Fl Abt (A) 237* crewed by Ltn Hoffmann and Gefr Tewes. Ball reported that after both adversaries had run out of ammunition, they flew alongside each other, laughing, until the German pilot waved and flew east. Ball commented: 'he was a real sport, that Hun'. Ball's report of this incident is curious, as his fire had killed Hoffmann, the observer, and seriously wounded Tewes.

Flt Sgt Tom Sharp gave a vivid picture of Ball at this time. In 1935 he recalled: 'I saw him more than once during September 1916, set off at dawn when the HA had sounded, clad only in pyjamas and come back an hour or more later, so stiff that we were almost frightened to lift him out of the cockpit for fear of breaking him, but always the same smile and either one or two fingers held up.'

More balloon attacks were ordered on 26 September. Roderic Hill flamed one with rockets over Boisleux-au-Mont at 1120 hrs, but

2Lt George Philippi. Philippi was wounded by anti-aircraft fire on 26 September 1916 (*M O'Connor*)

although Philippi flamed another over Bapaume, ten minutes later, he was wounded by ground fire, a bullet grazing his head. He managed to land back at Savy, but was unconscious when the mechanics lifted him from his cockpit, and he was taken to hospital.

The weather was deteriorating on 28 September, with hazy conditions, but patrols were flown during the evening. Ball and Ernest Foot patrolled together, Foot flying his Spad. Ball was the first to score, crashing an Albatros two seater at Haplincourt at 1745 hrs, but Foot soon followed. Twenty five minutes later, over Avesnes-les-Bapaume, he shot down an Albatros C Type from a formation of four, the first victory to be scored by an RFC Spad. This Albatros was from *Fl Abt* 238, crewed by Ltn Waler and Uffz Schendler, both wounded. Ball finished the day, forcing two more Albatros two-seaters to land: the first at 1915 hrs, at Bapaume, the second 15 minutes later north-east of the town.

On 29 September the remaining 80 hp Morane Bullets were returned to No 2 Aeroplane Supply Depot (2ASD). The unit's strength was now ten Nieuports and six 110 hp Bullets.

The last day of the month saw a great deal of fighting. The day was fine and warm and the Nieuports and Bullets, with FEs from No 11 Sqn, provided an escort in the morning for Nos 12 and 13 Sqn BEs bombing Lagnicourt, the base of *Jasta* 2. Nine enemy fighters came up to attack the British force. In the fighting, Ball and the crew of one of the FEs shared an Albatros C Type destroyed; Stanley Vincent flamed an Albatros D type, which crashed at Villers au Flos, killing Ltn Diener of *Jasta* 2; Bell-Irving claimed two Rolands crashed at the same location, and Walters drove down an Albatros over Bapaume. On the debit side, Manfred von Richthofen shot down an FE of No 11 Sqn for his third victory, and Capt Eustace Grenfell was forced to return with a badly shot up Bullet.

In an evening patrol, Ball attacked a formation of eight Rolands over Bapaume, sending one down out of control over Graincourt at 1830 hrs; 15 minutes later he attacked the same formation again, shooting another down out of control over Cambrai.

AN ACE DEPARTS

The first day of October was Ball's final day of operations with No 60 Sqn. Flying Nieuport A213 for the last time, Ball took off at 0720 hrs. Finding no hostile machines up, he flew to Lagnicourt and circled over the enemy aerodrome. Three enemy fighters took off to attack him. With the advantage of height, Ball went down to 500 ft and fired at the first from 30 yards. The enemy pilot hurriedly landed, his companions making off. Ball climbed back to 8000 ft and found an Albatros two-seater over Hamelincourt and forced it to land. He next attacked an all white Albatros two-seater, but after firing only 50 rounds his gun jammed. The Albatros landed in a field near Hamelincourt.

These victories were Ball's last in No 60 Sqn. To his 11 victories with No 11 Sqn he had added another 20 while with the unit. His official score was 31 victories, making him the most successful pilot of the RFC. On 3 October Ball made his goodbyes to the squadron,

On his return home Ball received a great deal of press coverage, the first British pilot to be given any official public acknowledgement of his achievements. In this photograph he is holding his famous red-painted spinner. In November 1916 Ball was awarded a second bar to his DSO. Returning to France on 7 April 1917 as a Flight commander in No 56 Sqn, Ball scored another 13 victories while with the unit, bringing his total to 44 before he was killed in action on 7 May 1917. Ball was awarded a posthumous Victoria Cross (VC) in June 1917

presenting his gramophone and records to his mechanics, a token of his appreciation of their hard work. Ball's favourite record was Schubert's 'Unfinished Symphony'. Sgt Maj A Nicod recalled: ' I often spoke to him about music, and was the proud possessor of some of his records'. At Ball's departure Douglas Latta was promoted to captain and took over command of A Flight.

The weather was now bad and during this period of inactivity C Flight began to exchange its 110 hp Bullets for Nieuports. However, there was to be one last Bullet casualty. On 17 October, Lt N McL Robertson, who had been posted in the previous day, took off with William Fry to intercept enemy aircraft reported over Gommecourt. There was heavy cloud, no enemy aeroplanes were seen, and the two Bullets became separated. Short of fuel, Robertson attempted to land at Hesdigneul aerodrome, but came in too fast, down wind, ran into a wood on the

The unsung heroes – B Flight goundcrew. Left to right: Sgt Roger, Flt Sgt Nicod, Sgt Hoskins. When asked 'Were a fitter and rigger allocated to you personally?' Chidlaw-Roberts replied, 'Yes, most certainly. We became great friends. When I had a Flight I had the same Flight sergeant and Corporal, in fact when I left 60 Sqn we wept together, my sergeant and I. We had become very fond of each other. They worked like devils, never grumbled, they were absolutely marvellous and we had all the honour and glory'

2Lt Roderic Hill joined No 60 Sqn in September 1916 and served with the unit for six months. Like his near contemporary Foot, Hill was an excellent aerobatic pilot. He is seen here as a Major in 1919, and rose to become Air Chief Marshal Sir Roderic Hill KCB MC AFC

edge of the field and was killed. Two days later the last of the 110 hp Bullets, Fry's A199, was replaced. None was sorry to see them go. Fry commented: 'It was difficult to keep one's head when so frightened of these machines, but essential, because if you panicked even for a minute you were in trouble…. I for one was only too glad to see the end of the Bullets.' Fry was convinced that the only reason there had not been even more casualties in the Bullets was because the unit had some of the finest pilots then in the RFC: Armstrong, Smart, Vincent, Meintjes and Hill.

On 19 October, C Flight flew its first two OPs in its Nieuports, but saw no action. Two days later A Flight flew an escort for a raid on Lagnicourt aerodrome. Bell-Irving fought a Roland two-seater, but his gun jammed, and the Roland crew shot through the petrol tank of his Nieuport, stopping his engine, and damaging one wing. Bell-Irving

Capt Alan Duncan Bell-Irving. A Canadian from Vancouver, Bell-Irving served as an observer in No 7 Sqn before training as a pilot. He was posted to No 60 Sqn in May 1916 and scored seven victories, including one balloon. He was wounded and shot down on 9 November 1916 and invalided back to England (*M O'Connor*)

force landed only 50 yards from the front line and the Nieuport was destroyed by enemy artillery.

On 26 October, a B Flight patrol, led by Capt Foot, took off at 1405 hrs. Eight Albatros D IIs from *Jasta* 2, led by Oswald Boelcke, were seen attacking four BE 2cs from Nos 5 and 15 Sqns near Ancre. Foot led the Nieuports into the action, but was outmanoeuvred by an enemy scout flown by Ltn Hans Imelmann, and his Lewis gun was hit. Foot dived away, but Imelmann attacked again, hitting the Nieuport's petrol tank and setting it on fire. Side slipping to keep the flames away from his cockpit, Foot crashed near Serre at 1500 hrs, but was unhurt. Roderic Hill had both gun and engine trouble. He glided back over the lines with a dead engine, overturned in a shell hole near Beugny and sustained a nasty crack on the head. A third member of the patrol, the Canadian Lt William M Carlyle, was shot down and killed by Ltn Hans von Keudall of *Jasta* 1. Euan Gilchrist was the only member of the Flight to return safely to Savy.

On 3 November Leslie Foot left for Home Establishment (HE) and Capt Alan Duncan Bell-Irving was given command of B Flight. The next day, Ltn Imelmann again claimed a pilot of the unit, shooting down Lt J M J Spenser. Spenser had earlier wounded Ltn Erich König of *Jasta* 2 in combat over Adinfer Wood, but was later attacked by Ltn Manfred von Richthofen, Ltn Otto Höhne and Imelmann. Imelmann's fire wounded Spenser, who crashed near Douchy. He was taken POW but later died of his wounds and was buried at Moyenville.

The morning of 9 November saw a major engagement, with nearly 40 aircraft involved in the fighting. At 0800 hrs six Nieuports from No 60 Sqn and eight FE 2ds from No 11 Sqn were on a photo reconnaissance. An hour later, another ten FEs from No 11 Sqn, six DH 2s from No 29 Sqn and 12 Nieuports from No 60 Sqn took off to fly an escort for the BE 2c bombers of Nos 12 and 13 Sqns, bombing the ammunition dump and German HQ at Vaulx-Vraucourt. At 0900 hrs, soon after crossing the lines, a large formation of enemy fighters attacked the bombers and their escort as they approached the target area. The enemy tactics were effective, breaking up the formations. Duncan Bell-Irving led four Nieuports to attack enemy scouts fighting the BEs. In the intense fighting he drove down one – a Halberstadt – but was hit in the engine by another. He spun away, recovered, but while going to the aid of an FE he was attacked by another enemy scout, whose fire wounded him in his left thigh, set fire to his Very pistol cartridges, hit his engine and holed his petrol tank. Bell-Irving crash landed at Guedecourt, completely wrecking the Nieuport. He was sent back to hospital in England. Roderic Hill also saw a great deal of fighting. His machine was badly shot about but he managed to return to Savy. Captain James Latta later led a force of six Nieuports to escort the bombers home. He fought with several enemy scouts at 1000 hrs and his machine was badly damaged. Only Lt D'Urban Victor Armstrong was successful, claiming a Roland driven down over Bois d'Havrincourt. At 1500 hrs, C Flight, Lts Weedon, Meintjes, H G Smart and Fry, led by Armstrong, flew an escort for the FEs of No 11 Sqn. Meintjes was the only successful pilot, forcing an LVG to land near Lagnicourt at 1515 hrs.

On the morning of 16 November Maj Smith-Barry led a patrol of seven Nieuports. Just after 1000 hrs it attacked a large formation of Roland scouts and LVG two-seaters in the vicinity of Adinfer Wood. During the fighting Lt D H Bacon was shot down, possibly by Ltn von Keudel of *Jasta* 1. Having survived the morning fight, 2Lt H E Martin was later killed in a practice flight, stalling Nieuport A135 on take-off.

The Somme battles finally ground to a halt on 18 November. Although a thaw had turned the ground to a sea of mud, snow and blizzards followed, making fighting almost impossible and the ground attacks gradually petered out. There was no flying.

On 23 November, Douglas Latta was posted to HE and his Flight taken over by Capt George Parker. Parker was not destined to last long with the unit. At 0900 hrs on 27 November, he was shot down and killed over Miraumont by Albatros of *Jasta* 2. Ltn Voss and Ltn Müller of the *Jasta* each claimed a Nieuport shot down, but Parker was the only casualty.

Parker was the unit's last casualty in 1916. Bad weather curtailed flying during December, but there were several notable changes in the unit, including the loss of two Flight commanders. On 11 December Capt Euan Gilchrist, the A Flight commander, crashed during a test flight and suffered a broken left arm, a fractured ankle and a scalp wound. He was invalided home to England. Roderic Hill was given command of the Flight. Another Flight commander was also lost during the day. Eustace Grenfell and his Flight had attacked a two-seater and Lt K L Caldwell's fire had forced it to land behind the British lines at Dainville. Excited by this uncommon occurrence, the entire Flight attempted to land near the enemy machine. Three crashed, Grenfell so badly that he broke his ankle. 'Grid' Caldwell commented in his

This Nieuport 16 A125 was lost on 3 November 1916 when Lt J M J Spenser was shot down. Spenser was taken POW but later died of his wounds (*Bernard Klaeylée*)

Captain Euan Gilchrist. The A Flight commander, Gilchrist crashed during a test flight on 11 December 1916 and was invalided home to England. After a period of instructing at the School of Special Flying, Gilchrist returned to France in May 1918 to command No 56 Sqn

Pilots of C Flight, Savy, December 1916. Left to right: Lt A D Whitehead, Lt L S Weedon, Capt H Meintjes (Flt Com) Lt K L Caldwell, Capt A Binnie, Lt W M Fry. Fry recalled: 'We lived in Nissen huts on the very edge of the aerodrome with our own little mess and the CO Smith-Barry and the rest of the squadron rather left us to ourselves'

logbook: 'Hun pilot shot in foot and Hun observer badly wounded by bullets (2) and by explosion when he put machine on fire.' Grenfell was invalided home and Henry 'Duke' Meintjes was promoted to captain and given command of C Flight.

The unit's last action in 1916 was on 27 December. Escorting a formation of FEs of No 11 Sqn, A Flight was attacked by 12 enemy scouts. During the fighting, Roderic Hill was attacked by a persistent Albatros and forced to spin down for 2000 ft to shake it off. Vincent fought an all-red Albatros for some time until the enemy pilot dived away east. All the British machines returned safely. In the afternoon, B Flight flew a diversionary patrol with the DH 2s of No 29 Sqn. Lt G A H Pidcock fought with a red painted Albatros, but was forced to break off the action when the lower left wing of his Nieuport twisted in its socket during a dive, a common fault on the Nieuport.

Bad weather during the last three days of December stopped nearly all war flying. No 60 Sqn had now recovered from its bad start and, equipped with its Nieuports, was beginning to make a name for itself. Despite the high casualty rate during the year, morale was good. At the onset of winter, with weather restricting flying, off duty recreation was a priority. In charge of these activities was Sgt Maj Aspinall. Smith-Barry, who was an excellent musician, decided to form an orchestra, appointing Vincent its OC. Sgts Hoskins, Billam and Cpls Vivian and McCliffe played violins; Cpls Bunny and Woodward, cornets, and McPolden drums, with Sgt Maj Nicod on piano completing the personnel. Concert parties were also arranged, and an orchestral podium, decorated with bunting, was erected in the C Flight hangar. A boxing ring was also constructed and matches organised. Contestants were accepted from other squadrons, but A M Bourne of the unit was the hero of the event. The following day a gale tore the corrugated iron roof off one of No 13 Sqn's sheds, coming to rest across two of the No 60 Sqn sheds. Roderic Hill, Leslie Foot, and several others were excellent aerobatic pilots and they flew through the gap, to the delight of the watching crowd.

So ended 1916 and the unit's first seven months of operations. It had been a period of varying fortunes, with many casualties, but as was common throughout the RFC there was a great feeling of comradeship; sometimes a sense of peace, even beauty, amidst the horrors of war. Recalling those autumn days of 1916, Willie Fry wrote: 'God, what wonderful days those were, coming home just before dark in the autumn or winter evenings, all the other squadrons and machines drawing home to their aerodromes, all firing Very lights to guide them in'.

Maj Evelyn P Graves. Graves replaced Smith-Barry as commanding officer of the unit on 22 December 1916. He was shot down in flames and killed on 6 March 1917

Christmas 1916. The unit's Christmas card was designed by Roderic Hill, a talented artist. The nearest Nieuport, with the spinner, is Albert Ball's

1917 – A NEW YEAR AND NEW CHALLENGES

On 24 December, Robert Smith-Barry was sent home. He had been writing in very strong terms to Trenchard, complaining that the replacement pilots being received by the unit were so badly trained that with only a few hours of solo flying they had little enthusiasm for flying fast scouts. He advocated forming a flying school to improve training. Trenchard agreed, Smith-Barry was posted to Gosport, where he founded the School of Special Flying, and many pilots from No 60 Sqn later became instructors there.

Replacing Smith-Barry, the unit's third commanding officer was Maj Evelyn P Graves. Like Smith-Barry, Graves was also lame as a result of a flying accident. He had been a Flight commander in No 20 Sqn in early 1916, then CO of No 9 Reserve Sqn.

FILESCAMP FARM

For a great deal of January, the weather was bad, with low clouds, wind and rain, plus frequent snow showers, restricting flying. No 60 Sqn flew no patrols, being busy collecting machines from the depot. On 18 January, the unit moved back to Le Hameau, but this time

Filescamp Farm, January 1917

occupying the eastern side of the aerodrome, part of Filescamp Farm. The squadron evidently thought that it would be here for some time as considerable effort was made to improve the facilities. It was a miserable time. The icy conditions caused guns to freeze, engines refused to start and the iron-hard frozen ground caused excessive wear to the Nieuport tailskids. Even the small amount of flying held a danger of frostbite, despite liberal quantities of whale oil applied to unprotected parts of the face.

On 21 January weather conditions were better but hazy, and no patrols were scheduled. Most pilots were taking the day off in Amiens but a few were making practice flights in the vicinity of the aerodrome. To their astonishment a German Rumpler suddenly appeared out of the mist and landed. The Rumpler was from *KG4/KS24* and the crew had become lost. Oblt Schumacher, the observer, had earlier ordered his pilot, Vfw Thurau, to land so that he could attempt to ascertain their position. Unfortunately they were at Tinques, behind the British lines, and Schumacher was taken prisoner. Thurau hastily took off again, but still lost, landed at Le Hameau. Realising his mistake, and possibly fed up with the whole situation, he set fire to the Rumpler and was taken prisoner. He and his officer were later reunited at the aerodrome, Schumacher soundly remonstrating with Thurau on becoming lost. Schumacher was given tea in the Officers' Mess, with Thurau being entertained by the squadron's sergeants.

With the weather improving, the last week of the month saw a return to war flying, the unit flying regular patrols. On 23 January, Capt Meintjes claimed two Rumplers driven down; one at 1100 hrs and another at 1500 hrs, both over Bois d'Adinfer. At 1040 hrs the next day,

Mine hosts at Filescamp Farm. Monsieur Tetus and his son are pictured right, while Madame Tetus and her daughter are shown below

Nieuports of C Flight at Filescamp Farm, January/February 1917. The nearest Nieuport A6646 C5 was flown from 2ASD by Capt K L Caldwell on 28 January 1917. The airman standing in front of the fuselage is Sgt Day. Next in line is A131 C1, which was lost on 8 April. The last Nieuport is A274 C2, flown by Lt W M Fry

Vincent claimed an Albatros two-seater, crashed at Monchy-au-Bois, confirmed by Keith Caldwell. 27 January was a busy and productive day. Leading a morning patrol, Meintjes attacked a formation of Albatros two-seaters at 8500 ft over Hogeaste Wood, forcing down two. During the fighting, the engine of Caldwell's machine stopped and he was forced to glide back over the lines, landing only 100 yards behind the British trenches. German artillery were quick to spot a target and completely destroyed the Nieuport within 20 minutes. In an afternoon patrol, Meintjes and Weedon forced an Albatros two-seater to land at Bois de Biez at 1345 hrs and 15 minutes later forced another down at Gommecourt.

On 29 January, 'Duke' Meintjes, Caldwell – known throughout the RFC as 'Grid' because of his allusion to all aeroplanes as 'Grids'– and William Fry were a few miles behind the German lines, just east of Gommecourt, flying at 13,000 ft. Conditions were perfect. The Nieuports were in a sunlit, bright blue sky, large cumulus clouds below them. Suddenly, Meintjes saw eight Albatros scouts a few hundred feet below, the bright colours of the enemy scouts – 'all the colours of the rainbow and led by a blood-red plane' – showing up vividly against the snow-white cloud, their black crosses 'startlingly clear'. Meintjes manoeuvred into a favourable position with the sun at his back, then dived to attack the enemy formation. The three Allied pilots were unaware that they were attacking the experienced men of *Jasta* 11 flying their new Albatros D IIIs. Fry recalled that he had no time to feel fear as he followed Meintjes and Caldwell into the fight: 'All was chaos for a few seconds. Meintj shot one down in our first attack. I think we surprised them by coming round the side of a cloud.' Fry escaped with only a few bullet holes through his machine, 'after seeming to have an Albatros on my tail shooting at me every time I looked round'. Caldwell was attacked by several of the enemy, his machine riddled with bullets: 'Petrol and oil tank and other parts of Grid shot through by explosive bullets, so landed at 8 [Sqn]. Machine a write off.' Fry was of the opinion that they were fortunate to have escaped as lightly as they did. 'The speed and tempo of the fight was something none of us had experienced before and it was a foretaste of what air fighting was going to be like in the future.' Nearly 50 years later, writing to Fry from his native New Zealand, 'Grid' Caldwell recalled the fight. 'We were a happy gang with old Meintj as leader. I remember a pretty hectic little do, Meintjes, you and I had early in '17 when we changed a line patrol into an offensive patrol and ran into 8 good Hun Albatri led by a red fellow which could well have been our friend Richthofen. Meintj shot one down, I was chased home with a riddled Nieuport and you survived too. I remember the CO seemed happy about it and gave us his Crossley car and a day off.' Meintjes' victory in the fight was possibly Ltn Georg Simon of *Jasta* 11, who was wounded.

Henry 'Duke' Meintjes. A South African, Meintjes flew with the unit from May 1916 until February 1917, scoring four victories. He was promoted captain to command C Flight and was awarded an MC. Nearly 60 years later, Grid Caldwell remembered: 'What a great chap 'Duke' Meintjes was. Liked by all. He was my Flight commander in 60 for a while and we had a lot of fun. He was rather blind in the air and we used to point out enemy formations at times which he had not seen, sometimes a mistake, as he was prone to attack vigorously forthwith with little tactical advantage.' In April 1917 Meintjes returned to France as a Flight commander in No 56 Sqn, scoring four additional victories before he was shot down and wounded on 7 May. After the war Meintjes flew with Handley Page as a pilot in an effort to get an airline operating between Cape Town and Johannesburg. He died on 25 May 1949

Lt William Mays Fry. Born in November 1896, Fry went to France as a private in the London Rifle Brigade in November 1914, but was returned to England as under age in the spring of 1915. Commissioned in the Somerset Light Infantry he transferred to the RFC in December 1915. Having completed his pilot training he served in Nos 12 and 11 Sqns before being posted to No 60 Sqn on 1 October 1916. Fry flew two tours with the unit, the last as Bishop's deputy leader of C Flight, scoring five victories and winning an MC. Returning to France in October 1917, he flew Spads as a Flight commander in No 23 Sqn, then Sopwith Dolphins in No 79 Sqn. He survived the war with 11 victories. His autobiography, *Air of Battle* was published in 1974. Fry died in 1992

Keith Logan 'Grid' Caldwell. A New Zealander, Caldwell was posted to No 60 Sqn on 18 November 1916 and in February was promoted to captain. and made C Flight commander. On his posting to HE in October 1917, Caldwell had scored eight victories. A contemporary, Robert Chidlaw-Roberts, commented on Caldwell's popularity in the squadron, 'Everybody loved Grid, of course, he was marvellous.' Caldwell later commanded No 74 Sqn in 1918, bringing his total victories to 25. In the opinion of those who knew and flew with him, if he had been a better shot, his skill, dash, determination and sheer courage would have seen him become one of the highest, if not the highest scorer in the RFC/RAF. Many years later, aware of this view, Caldwell ruefully remarked. 'With 27 Huns I couldn't have been too bad a shot.' Caldwell died in Jan 1997, at 84½, 30 minutes after cranking his car and joking that it was time he handed in his flying kit

The next success came on 7 February. Meintjes drove down an LVG over Gommecourt, but it was seven days before another victory. On 14 February Capt Stookes, and Lts G A Giles and C Williams, sent an enemy machine down out of control over Souastre at 1240 hrs. The weather now deteriorated to such an extent that RFC Communiqué No 76 recorded: 'From February 18th to 24th inclusive, no service flying was possible owing to unfavourable weather.' A return to war flying on the first day of March saw Caldwell in action in the afternoon, attacking two Albatros scouts over Grandcourt. One went down through the cloud cover, but the other stayed to fight: 'the other one, with a streamer on, scrapped for about ten minutes. His machine was a little faster and a better climber than C5 but the pilot was not very bon.' Caldwell's Nieuport A6646 was marked C5.

On 6 March, the unit suffered its first casualties since the loss of Bacon the previous November. The two-seater squadrons were finding that the aggressive *Jagdstaffeln* pilots were making photo-reconnaissance work extremely difficult and some of the unit's Nieuports were fitted with cameras. On 6 March, 2Lt Philip Joyce had taken photographs of the area around Cambrai and was escorted back to the British lines by C Flight: Caldwell, Bower and Weedon. Reaching the supposed safety of the line, and within sight of their aerodrome at Filescamp Farm, the three escorts left Joyce, and returned to engage enemy aircraft they had seen earlier near Cambrai. When the Flight returned to Filescamp Farm they were astonished to learn that Joyce had not returned. His body was never recovered and his loss remained a mystery for many years, but recent research has suggested the possibility that he was brought down by Oblt Kummetz of *Jasta* 1, who claimed a 'Sopwith' one seater at Achiet-le-Grand, which is directly west of Cambrai, en route for the shortest way back to the front line for the Nieuports, but still some distance south-east of Filescamp Farm. During the day Maj Graves was leading a patrol of three Nieuports towards the lines when he saw an FE 2b being attacked by eight Albatros scouts from *Jasta* 1 south-west of Arras. Graves went to the aid of the FE, but his Nieuport burst into flames and crashed north of Rivière. Graves was the victim of Ofstvz Cymera of *Jasta* 1 who claimed a 'Sopwith' single-seater at Agny, which is just north of Rivière. The unit's replacement CO was Maj Alan John

Nieuport 17 A201 of A Flight at Izel-le-Hameau in January/February 1917. Left to right: H Hamer, H Kirton, G Smart. Albert Ball scored 11 of his 44 victories flying this Nieuport which he brought with him from No 11 Sqn on being posted to No 60 Sqn

Maj Alan J L Scott. Scott took command of the unit on 10 March 1917. He scored five victories and was awarded an MC before being wounded on 10 July 1917

Lt Stanley F Vincent flew with No 60 Sqn from June 1916 until February 1917. Another early pilot of the RFC, Vincent scored two victories with No 60 Sqn and was the first pilot of the unit to be credited with an enemy aircraft as 'crashed' (*M O'Connor*)

Lance Scott, a New Zealander. Scott was also lame. Having broken both legs while training as a pilot, he walked with two sticks and had to be helped into and out of his cockpit. Despite this, he was an aggressive and courageous fighter pilot, often flying alone.

On 9 March, the unit received two replacement pilots, both Canadian lieutenants, who had served together as observers in No 21 Sqn: William Avery Bishop and Denis Townesend. Bishop was to become the unit's most successful pilot, claiming 47 victories in six months and winning a Victoria Cross (VC), a remarkable achievement.

Lt A D Whitehead and 2Lt F Bower flew an escort duty to BE 2s on 11 March, but Bower turned back after an hour with engine trouble. Whitehead carried on alone and attacked an enemy machine near Bailleul. This was a decoy; he was jumped by four Albatros from *Jasta* 2 and sent down in flames by Werner Voss of the *Jasta* for his 15th victory.

Nieuports of A Flight in the winter of 1916/1917. Left to right: C S Hall, H Kirton, G O Smart. Hall and Smart were both shot down and killed on the afternoon of 7 April 1917 by *Jasta* 11. Smart, flying Nieuport A6645, was Manfred von Richthofen's 37th victory. Hall, in Nieuport 23 A6766, was a victim of either Karl Schäfer or Kurt Wolff. The second Nieuport 17 A6718 A3 was flown by D C G Murray on 27 June when he was shot down and taken POW by Kurt Wolff of *Jasta* 29

The weather was very changeable during March, again curtailing patrols. On 17 March it snowed all day, but Scott took a new pilot, Lt William E Molesworth, to view the lines. Molesworth wrote, 'We started off late in the afternoon, climbing to about 8000 ft. The view was wonderful the ground covered with a thin coating of snow, while far away one could see the incessant flashing of the guns near the battered old town of Arras. White clouds floated in the ground mist over the eastern horizon like giant icebergs, their tops tinged with a wonderful pink which one only sees in the air.'

The final week of the month was to bring a string of victories. During an afternoon patrol on 25 March, three pilots were successful. At 1700 hrs, Bishop claimed his first victory, an Albatros scout crashed north of St Leger, 2Lt A Binnie claimed another crashed at Mercatel, and Frank Bower claimed another as out of control over the village. On 28 March, the inherent fault in the wings of the Nieuports claimed a victim. 2Lt Challoner Caffyn was killed when the starboard wings of his Nieuport came off at 2500 ft during practice.

A patrol on 30 March saw two casualties. Jumped by ten Albatros of *Jasta* 2, Lt W P Garnett was killed by Ltn Kurt Wolff. Frank Bower was hit in the back by an explosive bullet, causing dreadful wounds, but holding in his intestines with one hand he managed to land behind the lines near Fouquières, climbed from his machine and walked 40 yards before collapsing. Bower was taken to hospital but died of his wounds the next day.

On 31 March, in morning actions between 0730 and 0855 hrs, five enemy machines were claimed. At 0730 hrs, Scott and Capt C T Black shared in the destruction of an Albatros D III, which crashed at Heninel, Bishop crashing another south of Gavrelle. Forty five minutes later, Molesworth and Alan Binnie forced a Rumpler to land south of

Queant and, at 0855 hrs, Binnie drove down an Albatros scout east of Roclincourt. To end the day Townesend claimed an unknown type over Arras during an evening patrol.

The opposition: Albatros scouts on Roucourt airfield in the spring of 1917. Manfred von Richthofen's Albatros is the second machine in the line

The *Jagdstaffeln* had inflicted heavy losses on the RFC during March, but in reality the number of fighters employed was relatively small. Most *Jasta* were still well below establishment in both pilots and aeroplanes. The nominal strength of a *Jasta* was 12 aeroplanes but some, recently formed, carried only seven aeroplanes and pilots on strength. The RFC had numerical superiority but it was not enough. The technical superiority of the German fighters and the ever-growing confidence of their pilots in exploiting their aircraft to their full potential amply compensated for their numerical inferiority.

BLOODY APRIL

In preparation for the coming battle of Arras, the RFC stepped up its operations on 4 April, five days before the commencement of the battle. The result was a further increase in casualties, in both the corps two-seater and army Wing fighter squadrons.

Weather conditions on the first day of the month were bad, with low cloud, wind and rain. Conditions the next day were little changed and most of the aerial activity took place in the morning. Four Nieuports of the unit took off at 0715 hrs: Lts C T Black, C S Hall and V F Williams, flying an escort for Molesworth, whose Nieuport was fitted with a camera. Half an hour after taking off they attacked a formation of Albatros scouts from *Jasta* 2 over Fontaine-les-Croisilles. One of the enemy scouts was sent down out of control by Hall, but Williams was attacked by Ltn Bernert, his Nieuport bursting into flames.

The air offensive for the battle of Arras opened on 4 April, but low clouds, wind and rain limited the amount of flying. Snow was also moving in from the east and was reported by several squadrons to be falling on their aerodromes. The unit's Nieuports had been fitted with Le Prieur rockets in anticipation of being ordered to attack kite balloons during the offensive and the first attacks were ordered on 5 April. Just after midday Bishop and E J D Townesend took off to attack two balloons near Cambrai. Bishop's target was not up, and Townesend was intercepted by *Jasta* 11. Accurate fire from Vfw Festner wounded Townesend in both legs and forced him to crash land behind the German lines. The young Canadian was thrown out of the cockpit on impact and taken prisoner. At the end of the day, a defensive patrol of six Nieuports, led by Lt Geoffrey Pidcock, attacked two enemy machines, one of which was a red Albatros, and sent one down out of control near Riencourt at 1845 hrs.

Just before 1500 hrs on 7 April, Bishop took off alone to attack a balloon at Ecourt St Quentin. As the Canadian began his dive he was intercepted by an Albatros, but he got behind it and a burst of fire sent it down. Bishop then resumed his attack on the balloon, diving to within 500 ft of the ground, the long dive choking and stopping his engine. Bishop prepared to make a forced landing behind enemy lines, but at 15 ft the engine restarted and he made for the British lines under intense ground fire. Both the balloon and the Albatros D III were awarded as destroyed. Bishop was awarded an MC for this action.

An offensive patrol, which left at 1640 hrs, was attacked by von Richthofen's *Jasta* 11 over Arras. In the intense fighting, Manfred von Richthofen shot down 2Lt George Smart, and Charles Hall was killed by Ltn Kurt Wolff for his seventh victory. Lt H E Hervey, whose guns had frozen, leaving him defenceless, was attacked by Vfw Festner, and hit in the engine, but he spun away and flew back to base. The Nieuport, badly damaged by Festner's fire, was returned to 2ASD. The Nieuports of both 2Lt D N Robertson and Lt John Elliot were badly shot up in the fighting, with Norman Robertson wounded in the hand.

Lt E J D Townesend was shot down and taken prisoner on 5 April 1917 in Nieuport 17 A6693 (*M O'Connor*)

Lt Geoffrey A H Pidcock. Known as 'Pidders' throughout the RFC, Pidcock served in No 60 Sqn from September 1916 until May 1917. He scored one victory with the unit with two more classified as driven down. From March to July 1918 he served in 73 Sqn as a Flight commander. He survived the war with six victories (*M O'Connor*)

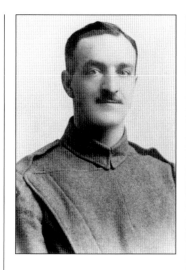

Lt George O Smart. Smart was shot down on 7 April 1917 by Manfred von Richthofen for his 37th victory (*M O'Connor*)

Nieuport 17 A311 C1 in a German dump. Lt H E 'Tim' Hervey was shot down by anti-aircraft fire on 8 April 1917 in this machine and taken prisoner (*M O'Connor*)

The next patrol was led by Capt Maurice Knowles, with Lts L H Leckie, Pidcock, H Kirton and T Langwill. Knowles failed to return. He was shot down by Ltn W Frankl of *Jasta* 4 for the last of his 20 victories. He was killed the next day in combat with the Bristol Fighters of No 48 Sqn.

It snowed heavily on 8 April, Easter Sunday. At 0835 hrs, Alan Scott led a patrol of five Nieuports, mainly C Flight pilots, on an OP to the area of Douai. Scott found an Albatros two-seater over the town and immediately attacked it, sending it down to crash. Albatros D IIIs from *Jasta* 11 now climbed to attack the British scouts, Vfw Festner shooting down French-Canadian, Major J A A Milot. Hervey broke off from the fight to clear a gun jam and found himself alone. Flying back to the lines his Nieuport was hit by Archie, shrapnel going through the bottom wing before ending up in the engine. With insufficient height to glide back over the British lines, Hervey force landed, on top of a well-camouflaged German artillery dugout. In his autobiography, *Cage-Birds*, Tim Hervey wrote. 'My machine was immediately surrounded and I was unceremoniously hauled out, head first, and was just beginning to think I was in for a rough house when two officers appeared.' The officers calmed their men and Hervey was taken to their billet and given lunch by the battery commander.

After the attack on the two-seater, Scott and Bishop became separated from the other Nieuports. Bishop attacked a balloon, which was hauled down, smoking. Bishop claimed two Albatros scouts in this patrol. The first out of control north-east of Arras at 0930 hrs; another destroyed in the vicinity of Vitry at 1010 hrs. The Canadian also claimed a two-seater driven down east of Arras at 0940 hrs.

Lt William Oswald Russell. Russell, a Londoner, was shot down and taken prisoner on 14 April 1917 by Manfred von Richthofen for his 44th victory (*N Franks*)

The battle of Arras began on the morning of 9 April. In support of the ground forces, the squadron was ordered to attack enemy troop movements, transport, and other targets of opportunity. The low flying which these duties entailed was unpopular with the pilots – the aggressive *Jasta* pilots were quick to exploit their height advantage – and it was with some relief that the unit was later returned to the usual OPs and escort patrols.

On 14 April, the FEs of No 11 Sqn flew a photographic reconnaissance in the vicinity of Douai and Capt Binnie led B Flight on a diversionary patrol. Binnie and Lt W Russell attacked a pair of hostile two-seaters over Douai, but return fire from one of the enemy observers hit William Russell's machine in the petrol tank, pouring fuel over his legs and stopping his engine. Albatros from *Jasta* 11 then appeared on the scene and shot down four Nieuports in quick succession. Manfred von Richthofen attacked the disabled Russell, who force landed and was taken prisoner. Alan Binnie was

attacked by Lothar von Richthofen, whose fire hit him in the left shoulder and set his Nieuport alight. Binnie fainted, but came to in time to land behind the lines. He was taken to hospital and his arm was later amputated. Lt Lewis Chapman, a Londoner, was shot down by Vfw Festner and taken prisoner, dying of his wounds two days later, and New Zealander John Cock was shot down and killed by Kurt Wolff for his 14th victory. Lt Graham Young was the only pilot to return from this disastrous patrol.

Worse was to come. *Jasta* 11 had not finished with the unit. Two days later, at 0915 hrs, the *Jasta* attacked six Nieuports of A Flight, led by 2Lt Pidcock. 2Lt R E Kimbell was shot down and killed by Kurt Wolff; Lothar von Richthofen fatally wounded Norman Robertson, who was taken POW; Australian Lt Trevor Langwill was forced to land and taken prisoner by Vfw Festner, but died of his wounds the next day, and the Canadian Lt J McC Elliot was shot down and killed. Only two British machines returned to Filescamp Farm: 2Lt L H Leckie

The hangars at Filescamp Farm. On the right, behind the sandbags, are the squadron offices (*L Rogers*)

and Pidcock, the latter claiming two Albatros as forced to land, one of which was possibly Festner.

The German fighter pilots were now exploiting to the full the advantages of their Albatros fighters, faster than the Nieuports and with double the fire power. With eight pilots lost in three days, Maj Scott called a halt to any further patrols until replacement aeroplanes were received and there was time to train the replacement pilots properly. Scott was conscious that, of the pilots lost on 14 April, only Capt Binnie had been with the unit for more than a few days.

Although bad weather for the next four days helped with the training of replacement pilots, it also curtailed flying practice, and on 20 April the unit returned to operations, Bishop claiming an Aviatik C type in flames at 1458 hrs over Biache-St-Vaast.

Over the previous few days enemy balloons had been closely observing the movements of the ground troops and Wing ordered they must be destroyed. Le Prieur rockets had been fitted to the Nieuports, but during practice these were considered ineffective. In a letter home, 'Moley' Molesworth graphically described these practice attacks, 'One dives at a target on the ground and when within fifty yards of it presses a button on the instrument board. Immediately there is a most awful hissing noise, which can be heard above the roar of the engine and six huge rockets shoot forward from the struts each side towards the target. We did not think these were much of a success, owing to the difficulty of hitting anything, so decided to use tracer and Buckingham bullets instead.'

On 22 April Lts G L Lloyd, Molesworth, H Ross, Cyril Patteson and A R Penny all destroyed balloons. Molesworth was in the middle of writing a letter when orders to attack them came through. 'I will finish this when I come back if old Fritz doesn't stop me.' 'Old Fritz' didn't stop him. Two hours later he continued the letter: 'Here I am, back again with a Hun and a "sausage" added to my bag. I am fearfully bucked with life, as the Major has just told me I have been made a flight commander.' During the morning, Bishop claimed two Albatros scouts shot down at 1120 hrs over Vis-en-Artois and in the afternoon patrols, Patteson crashed an Albatros at Vitry at 1720 hrs and Molesworth another out of control. To round off the day's successes, Scott, leading an evening patrol, drove down an Albatros C Type and a scout at 1845 hrs over Biache-St-Vaast.

On 23 April Bishop claimed his tenth and eleventh victories: an Albatros C III forced to land at Vitry-en-Artois at 1530 hrs and an Albatros scout destroyed east of Vitry at 1559 hrs. The following day, Scott led a morning patrol of five Nieuports, Molesworth flying in the rear of the formation. Crossing the lines at 10,000 ft, the British scouts were flying towards towards Douai when they saw a patrol of Sopwith 1½ Strutters from No 70 Sqn under attack from Albatros scouts of *Jasta* Boelcke. Molesworth saw one British two-seater go down in flames, 'the poor devils going down burning like a furnace'. Scott immediately led the Nieuports down to attack the enemy scouts. Molesworth later wrote, 'I knew that I was in for my first real big scrap. The leader saw us coming and turned east with his nose well down. However, we soon caught him up and started scrapping. I managed to get well behind a Hun two-seater, which was a little way out of the scrap. He didn't seem to mind me plugging him a bit, and went calmly on. In my excitement I lost my head and started to spin madly to the ground.' This two-seater was known to the pilots of the unit as the Flying Pig, 'owing to the likeness of the observer to that rotund animal'. Coming out of

Bishop demonstrates for the press the use of the Lewis gun to fire upwards. In the interests of safety the Lewis gun was not allowed to be cocked in the down position until ready to be used. Before the gun could be fired the pilot had to pull down the gun and cock it. To solve this problem, Technical Sgt Maj Smyrk – described by Maj Scott as 'a wizard with an internal combustion engine' – designed a cocking handle which enabled the pilot to reach up and cock the gun without having to pull it down

Capt William Earle Molesworth. 'Moley' Molesworth served in No 60 Sqn from March to August 1917. In May he was promoted to captain and given command of A Flight. He scored six victories with the unit and was awarded an MC. In October he was posted to No 29 Sqn and gained another 12 victories, bringing his total to 18

his spin, Molesworth saw an Albatros scout 50 yards ahead of him. 'So I loosed off at him and saw him spin and crash on the ground, much to my delight.'

After lunch, attacks on balloons were ordered. Molesworth was successful, flaming one over Boiry Notre Dame at 1305 hrs, but while firing at his balloon, Clark was attacked by four Albatros scouts and hit in both legs, breaking one. Clark flew back to the front lines at only 50 ft, harassed by the enemy pilots. As he was crossing the enemy trenches, the Nieuport was hit in the petrol tank, setting it on fire. Clark landed on the British side, managed to avoid numerous shell holes, but ran into a trench, which put the Nieuport up onto its nose. Men from a nearby dressing station ran to the scene and pulled Clark from the burning machine. Although badly burnt, the Australian insisted on making his report before allowing a doctor to treat his injuries. He died of his wounds on 1 May.

On 27 April, Bishop destroyed a balloon over Vitry-en-Artois, and two days later, now promoted to captain, he destroyed a Halberstadt east of Epinoy at 1155 hrs. On the last day of the month Bishop claimed three Albatros C IIIs, one crashed and two forced to land.

During the month the unit had claimed 31 enemy machines and nine balloons, but the last four days of the month had seen more casualties. 2Lt N D Henderson was hit by anti-aircraft fire, crashed into a lake near Fampoux and seriously injured; 2Lt Stedman, collecting a Nieuport from Candas, became lost, landed behind the German lines and was taken prisoner, and 2Lt Hubert 'Tiny' Ross sustained a broken leg, cuts and bruises when the wings of his Nieuport came off while diving onto a practice ground target. There was another instance of structural failure on 30 April: Arthur Penny's Nieuport lost its lower port wing during a dive on hostile aircraft. Penny managed to return, crashing just east of Arras. Molesworth witnessed the incident: 'We had our noses down, going full out to try and catch the blighters, when suddenly the Hun directly under us did a sharp turn. The chap on my right yanked his grid over after him. He pulled her over with such a jerk that one of his bottom planes came off and fluttered down to the ground in two bits. I couldn't see what happened to him after that as we were getting to close quarters with the Huns.' On landing Molesworth reported that Penny had 'gone west' as he had seen his machine break up in mid air. 'Hardly had I finished when, to my amazement, he appeared outside the window. I could not believe my eyes and thought it was his ghost, but he turned out to be flesh and blood and so we went to the mess and had a drink on the strength of it.'

During Bloody April, No 60 Sqn had lost 18 pilots, a casualty rate of 100 per cent, and it was to be another two months before the unit was re-equipped with the SE 5 and able to meet the German Albatros scouts on equal terms in respect of speed and, more importantly, fire power.

William Fry opened the scoring in May. Flying a morning escort patrol on 2 May, he forced an Albatros to land over Drocourt-Vitry, but during the combat the right hand bottom wing of his Nieuport broke free from its strut fixing. His machine went into a spin, but Fry

Capt William Avery Bishop with Nieuport 23 B1566. While serving in No 60 Sqn, Bishop scored 29 of his 47 victories in this Nieuport (*M O'Connor*)

managed to recover and flew back to Filescamp Farm. Maj Scott commented in his report to Wing: 'This is the fourth Nieuport Scout to break in the air in 35 days. Luckily Lt Fry is a good and fearless pilot.' In the same patrol, Bishop claimed two Albatros C IIIs destroyed for his 15th and 16th victories. After returning from this patrol, while having lunch, a pair of hostile two-seaters were reported as working over the lines. Leaving their meal, Bishop and Fry flew to the lines and attacked the enemy machines, pointed out to them by British anti-aircraft batteries. Bishop claimed one as destroyed, but the other cleared east. When they returned their lunches had been saved, still hot. They had been only an hour in the air. In a day of continued success, an evening patrol claimed three victories: an Albatros scout out of control over Drocourt by Fry; another crashed by Lt S B Horn over Vitry-Belonne, and Maj Scott crashed another scout over Éterpigny.

On 4 May, Bishop and Fry claimed an AEG CV destroyed over Brebieres-Vitry at 1330 hrs. On 6 May an escort patrol, led by Spenser Horn, was attacked at 1800 hrs by Albatros of *Jasta* 5. During the fighting, Horn sent an Albatros down out of control over Cambrai, but two Canadian pilots were forced down and taken POW. 2Lt C W McKissock was claimed by Offstv Nathanael for his 15th victory and 2Lt Gordon D Hunter was badly wounded and taken prisoner by Ltn Schneider.

In addition to his duties as C Flight commander, Bishop was now flying lone patrols and on 7 May he claimed two Albatros scouts. The next day he went on leave, entrusting the command of the Flight to Fry. On 8 May, firing at a ground target on the aerodrome, Fry experienced yet another wing failure, but safely landed the Nieuport.

2Lt G D Hunter. Hunter was wounded and shot down on 6 May 1917. His left arm was later amputated. He is seen here in a German POW camp. Although he signed this photograph as 'C4', photographs of his captured Nieuport show that it was marked C6 (*M O'Connor*)

On 11 May, Fry led the patrol in actions which were to win him an MC. In the evening, British infantry of Third Army were to mount an offensive near Roeux. Orders from Wing specified that enemy trenches and positions should be attacked as the troops went over the top, and watches were carefully synchronised with those of Third Army HQ. These duties were allocated to FE 2bs of No 11 Sqn and Nieuports of No 60 Sqn, led by Fry, who recalled that these attacks required a great degree of accuracy, both in the timing and their location. Ordinary maps were of no use due to the devastated nature of the terrain, a mass of shell holes and trenches, and the pilots had to rely on the study of aerial photographs. Before the attack, five Nieuports flew to and fro above the front lines. Everything was quiet. Then, at five minutes before zero hour, the artillery began their barrage, compounded by return fire from the German batteries. Fry later wrote:

'The thought of having to shortly dive down into the middle of it all was not pleasant. I looked round to see the others following me in close formation. Then, at the exact moment, we turned parallel to the lines, peeled off and dived one after the other, concentrating our fire on the German trenches as shown on the maps we had studied so carefully. The sky must have been teeming with shells and before we dived we all caught sight of some in the air and now and then saw the curve of the top of the trajectory of some of them.'

Hunter's Nieuport 23 B1597 C6 surrounded by German personnel

A fine shot of B1597 under a more relaxed guard (*C Huston*)

Nieuport 23 B1514 A4 was shot
down and captured on 6 May 1917.
The pilot, 2Lt C W McKissock, was
taken prisoner (*M O'Connor*)

After capture, B1514 was taken
to the base of *Fl Abt* 7. Seen here
under the supervision of Uffz Paul
Baeumer, a pilot in *Fl Abt* 7, it is
being repaired and repainted with
German markings

Going down to 300 ft the pilots selected their targets, using a railway
cutting as a guide. Reaching the end of the target area they turned and
renewed their attacks. 'The din was tremendous and we were bumped
about by air disturbance caused by shells passing near by.' The pilots
turned off individually to change their Lewis gun drums – 'there was
no question of replacing the empty ones in the cockpit, they just went
overboard.' Exhilarated by the success of their attacks, but with their
ammunition exhausted, the pilots flew straight back to Filescamp Farm,
a short flight of only a few minutes. Rearmed with fresh Lewis gun

drums, and with Scott's approval and encouragement, they went back to renew their attacks. Even more care was now needed as it was not certain which of the enemy trenches the British troops had taken, and the Nieuports attacked only those trenches further back, which they knew the troops could not possibly have reached. They again used all their ammunition and returned without loss. It was nearly dark as the last Nieuport landed back at Filescamp Farm.

On 13 May, Fry destroyed an Albatros scout over Dury at 1430 hrs, but there were no further actions until 18 May. B Flight were in action in the morning with enemy two-seaters near Remy. As 2Lt Richard J Grandin dived to attack one, both wings of his Nieuport broke off and he was killed. 2Lt Eric S Howard was also killed during the day, when he spun in from 100 ft.

There was an unusual victory on 19 May. The pilots were preparing to set off on a morning patrol, either sitting in their Nieuports or standing nearby, when they were astonished to see an Albatros suddenly appear out of the cloud, 1000 ft above the aerodrome: 'there was considerable excitement with mechanics running about and pointing upwards.' The German pilot realised his mistake and quickly climbed back into the cloud cover. Those pilots who were not yet in their machines hurriedly climbed into their cockpits. One pilot, a Scot named Graham Young, was so excited that in his hurry he forgot to wave for his chocks to be taken away from under his wheels before he opened up his engine. The tail of the Nieuport immediately went up, it stood on its nose, then went over onto its back. The other pilots took off and flew up through the cloud looking for the enemy scout. Fry finally spotted it and gave chase, firing a few bursts, 'but too excited at first to take proper aim through the sight.' The Albatros pilot, Ltn Georg Noth of *Jasta* B, decided that discretion was the better part of valour and crash landed in the nearest open space, turning the Albatros over. Both Noth and Fry were very low and Fry pulled up sharply to avoid a collision. He landed close by, ran to the scene of the crash and shook hands with Noth, who admitted that he had become lost. A battalion of Somerset Light Infantry – Fry's regiment before he had been seconded to the RFC – who were in rest nearby, surrounded the Albatros and their adjutant telephoned for a car to be sent for Noth to be taken back to Filescamp Farm. Fry flew back. Noth was given lunch in the Mess, where he was plied with drink, but he said very little and gave nothing away, although he did volunteer the information that he was with *Jasta* B, and a Cambrai theatre ticket was found in his tunic for the previous night's performance. Fry later commented: 'the whole affair was no achievement on my part as it was pure luck to come across him in the clouds, there was no fight, and once I got on his tail he gave up.'

The next day, Fry again led C Flight in ground strafing operations, well behind the lines at Fontaine-les-Croisilles. On 25 May he had yet

Two views of Ltn Georg Noth's Albatros D796/17 after being forced to land on 19 May 1917. Noth's Albatros was designated G 39 and sent to England for evaluation (*G van Wyngarden*)

another wing failure, the lower starboard wing of the Nieuport breaking off, and he was forced to land. The same day saw the return of 'Grid' Caldwell to operations. He had been taken ill while on leave and had been absent from the squadron since 6 March. In a morning patrol, 20 enemy machines were seen and there was some spasmodic, inconclusive fighting before five Albatros scouts of *Jasta* 5 attacked a Bristol Fighter which had joined the patrol. 2Lt Warren Gilchrist was singled out by Ltn Allmenroder, wounded, forced to land, and taken POW. In morning patrols the next day, Fry forced down an Albatros scout over Monchy and Caldwell and 2Lt W H Gunner shared in another, out of control over Belonne. Bishop had returned from leave and claimed his 20th victory with an Albatros scout out of control over Izel-les-Epeurchin. On 27 May Lts Gunner and R U Phalen forced down a pair of two-seaters over Biache, possibly from *Fl Abt (A)* 288 which lost two crews in the area.

2Lt Warren Gilchrist, the brother of Euan Gilchrist, in a POW camp. He was shot down on 25 May 1917

Caldwell, now a captain, had been given command of B Flight on his return, and on 28 May was leading an OP. Joined by a Bristol Fighter the British force chased nine Albatros scouts towards Lens. Two of the patrol fell out with technical trouble, the Bristol was left behind, and Caldwell and Phalen attacked alone. Phalen was shot down and killed by Ltn Schuhmann of *Jasta* 5 for his fifth victory. After fighting a pair of two-seaters, Caldwell was attacked by three enemy scouts. One, coloured red and black and flying streamers, was flown by an exceedingly skilful pilot, who outmanoeuvred Caldwell and badly damaged his Nieuport. Caldwell wrote in his logbook: '…was attacked by three scouts from behind. One with streamers was hot stuff and I couldn't shake him off until down to 200 ft. My petrol tank, flying wires, aileron control, struts and main tank, all shot through, so I came home after a brief scrap with another two scouts who were pretty dud.' Caldwell landed at the nearest aerodrome, La Bellevue. His Nieuport was 'like a sieve; hence, a new Nieuport.' Although an Allied anti-aircraft battery reported this Albatros as being flown by the German ace, Ltn Voss, an opinion shared by Caldwell, it could equally have been Ltn Kurt Schneider who is known to have flown a red and black Albatros.

On 28 May, Maj Scott was out early, flying a solo patrol. A patrol of SEs from No 56 Squadron were also in Scott's area and two of their number had gone down to attack a pair of two-seaters working at 4000 ft, the rest of the patrol staying up to engage two formations of scouts, between 13 or 15 in number, which were at their level. Suddenly, Scott, coming from the direction of Douai, dived into the enemy scouts, got in a good burst 'at very close range ' then zoomed up to join the SEs.

The combined British force then attacked the enemy formation. Scott shot down one of the enemy scouts, and pilots from No 56 Sqn claimed one out of control and another forced to land. Despite the fierceness of the fighting these were the only positive results. Scott's Nieuport had been considerably shot about and he was forced to land behind the British lines. He telephoned the squadron, then borrowed a horse from an artillery ammunition column to get to the nearest road, where he rendezvoused with the squadron car which had been sent to fetch him. The reason for Scott's haste was that he was anxious to shave and change out of his flying clothes before an inspection of the squadron by General Allenby, GOC of Third Army, and the Brigade and Wing Commanders, due at 0900 hrs. In his combat report of this action, under the heading 'Duty', Scott wrote: 'Recreational.'

The Canadian Billy Bishop rounded off the month on the last day with an Albatros scout destroyed over Epinoy at 0700 hrs. It had been a good month for the unit: 28 victories had been claimed for the loss of five pilots. June would prove to be even better, with only two pilots lost against a victory tally of 19 victories.

A VC RAID

At 0357 hrs on 2 June, Bishop took off alone. His intention was to attack an enemy aerodrome. The weather was bad, with low cloud and drizzle, but it improved as he neared the front lines. At 0415 hrs he

Billy Bishop with 'Richthofen,' the squadron's piglet. This long suffering little porker was at different times painted with either a red, white and blue roundel or with German Maltese crosses on its back and ears, plus a streamer on its tail

arrived over what he thought was the enemy aerodrome at Anneux. There was no activity on the ground and no worthwhile targets, so he flew on. The next aerodrome was seen by chance; Bishop later believed that it was either Esnes or Awoignt. Several Albatros scouts were lined up on the field, plus a two-seater. There were four sheds, a large hangar and vehicles parked on the boundary road. Some of the enemy scouts had their engines running. Bishop attacked these, then switched his attention to one which had taken off. He shot this down with a 30 round burst. A second Albatros was now airborne, but the Canadian dispatched this with another 30 rounds from 150 yards range, the enemy machine crashing into some trees near the field. Two more Albatros had now taken off and were gaining height. Bishop climbed to 1000 ft and fired at one, finishing his ammunition drum. Replacing his empty drum, Bishop turned on the other and fired a complete drum at it, causing it to turn away. He then saw that four enemy machines were above him at 5000 ft and he made for home. He flew below the enemy machines for about a mile, heading south, before turning west. Crossing the lines, but unsure of his whereabouts, Bishop landed to ascertain his position. This done, he flew back to Filescamp Farm, landing at 0540 hrs. As a result of this action, although entirely unwitnessed, Bishop was awarded a VC, the recommendation going through unusual channels, bypassing RFC chain of command, and going straight from Maj Scott to Capt Lord Dalmeny, the GOC's Assistant Military Secretary, who was a personal friend of Scott, then to General Allenby. It must be said that there are no German reports

Capts W J Rutherford and W Bishop, photographed in the summer of 1917

of any aerodrome being attacked on 2 June 1917 or of aircraft losses. In 1995, noted Canadian researcher, the late Philip Markham, made an intensive study of Bishop's report in an attempt to ascertain the aerodrome which Bishop may have attacked. He concluded. 'I have been unable to discover any supporting evidence; in fact it has been quite the reverse.'

On 5 June, Scott shot down an Albatros over Monchy at 2035 hrs for his 9th victory. Ltn Oscar von Schickfuss und Neudorff of *Jasta* 3, with his *Jasta* compatriot, Vfw Wilhelm Reiss, were attacking a Nieuport of No 40 Sqn when Scott intervened, shooting down Neudorff in the British lines. Neudorff's Albatros D III was designated as G 43.

The structural weakness of the Nieuport wing claimed another victim on 7 June. 2Lt Roland Harris was flying a ground to air firing practice when both starboard wings of his machine broke away. The Nieuport dived straight into the ground and Harris was killed.

When the battle of Messines opened on 7 June, the main fighting was now further north and activity over the front of III Army was reduced. An Aeroplane Intercepting Station had been set up by 13th Wing, which could obtain a fix on enemy observation aeroplanes and pilots of the unit were ordered to take off in pairs to intercept them. In addition to their normal patrols this meant that pilots were on standby, sometimes for considerable periods of time. Added to this was the frustration that the enemy machines usually saw the British scouts, escaping east over their rear areas before they could be intercepted, only to return when the RFC scouts had left. On 15 June, possibly as a

The wreckage of Lt D R C Lloyd's Nieuport 23 No.B1610, after his fatal collision with Vfw Robert Riessinger of *Jasta* 12 on 16 June 1917 (*G Van Wyngarden*)

result of this frustration, Bishop led 15 Nieuports over the German aerodrome at Epinoy, in a challenge to the *Jasta* pilots. Lt David Lloyd commented: 'We must have looked like a bunch of berserk eagles. We should have charged the Huns admission.'

In the evening of 16 June, eight Nieuports flew an OP: Caldwell leading B Flight with Fry leading C Flight above. Caldwell's formation was attacked by five Albatros scouts, but C Flight dived and drove them down through the lower Flight, with Fry, Graham Young, W J Rutherford and Lloyd forcing two Albatros down from 11,000 to 3000 ft. During the fierce fighting, 'Red' Lloyd collided with an enemy scout flown by Vfw Robert Riessinger of *Jasta* 12. Both pilots were killed. Ltn Hermann Becker of the *Jasta* was wounded and shot down by Caldwell.

During the next ten days, nine victories were claimed for no loss. Lts Pope and Penny shared an Albatros scout out of control on 20 June, with W E Jenkins, J Collier and R B Steele, claiming an Albatros C type the next day. On 24 June, Bishop claimed an Albatros scout, flamed over Beaumont, and an evening patrol by B Flight claimed two more victories: Caldwell crashed a scout and shared another out of control with D C G Murray and Alexander Adam. On 26 June, Bishop claimed an Albatros D III, flamed over Annay and another out of control for his 30th victory.

Caldwell led an evening patrol on 27 June. Attacking three enemy Albatros at 8000 ft over Beaumont, the Nieuports were jumped by another eight and Murray was wounded, shot down and taken POW by Ltn Kurt Wolff, Staffelführer of *Jasta* 29, for his 31st victory.

The remains of Riessinger's Albatros
G Van Wyngarden

Doubles on the tennis court at Filescamp Farm. The pilot on the far right, wearing strange headgear for a tennis match, is 'Poppy' Pope

In the evening of 29 June, Capt Molesworth, leading a combined force of A and B Flights, attacked eight enemy scouts between Douai and Cambrai. In a letter home the next day he graphically described the actions:

'Yesterday I had the narrowest shave I've ever had since I started Boche-strafing. I was properly caught out this time and really thought

Lt Sydney L G 'Poppy' Pope (left) with Lt A R Penny. Penny was wounded in action on 5 August 1917 while serving with No 29 Sqn (*L Rogers*)

things were all up. We were over the Drocourt Switch, near Vitry, when a dozen Huns got what you might call "uppish". We tumbled into a proper mix up and, as there were only five of us, the Huns managed to break up our formation. We had arranged that if this should happen we were to return to the line independently and reform, so I started towards Arras, following the Scarpe. Just as I was passing over Gravelle I espied three fat Hun two-seaters making south east. "Here we are, my son," says I to myself. "We'll just hop down and put the gust up one of these Huns." No sooner said than done, I pushed my nose down and, when within range, opened fire. The next thing I knew was a perfect hail of bullets pouring round me. Here is a rough description of my thoughts during the next few minutes that followed. Crackle! Crackle! Crackle! My cheery aunt! There's a Hun on my tail. By Jove! The blighter is making my grid into a sieve. Confound him! Let's pull her up in a good climbing turn and have a look at him. Heavens! It's the Circus. I wonder if old Richthof is the leader. The dirty dog nearly caught me out this time. Silly ass, didn't hold his fire long enough or he'd have made me cold meat by now. Let's give him a dose and see how he likes it. Here he comes, straight at me, loosing off with both guns. I hope we aren't going to collide. Missed! Bon! Everything's A1. Wish I'd hit him though. I must pull her round quick or he'll be on my tail. Hang! I can't shoot for toffee, but he's pretty dud too, thank heavens. Once again boys, round with her. Let him have it hot. No good. Try again. Confound it, there's my beastly drum empty. I must spin and change it. Good enough. Now, where's the blighter? My Harry. He has got me stiff this time, here he comes down on me from the right. Crack! Crack! Crack! Bang! Zip! Zip! There goes my petrol tank; now for the flames. Cheero! No luck this time, you old swine. Wait till I get you next show. Here goes for the ground. Luckily for me my friend and his pals, who had been watching the scrap, thought I was done for. They therefore chucked up the sponge and departed. I managed to pull the machine out, just scraping over the trenches. The engine was still running, although the petrol was pouring out all over my legs. A few minutes afterwards the engine conked out altogether, and I had to land in a field. I was immediately surrounded by a crowd of men, who had seen the fight. Amongst them were some

Lt D C G Murray was wounded, shot down and taken prisoner on 27 June 1917. His Nieuport 17 A6718 A3 is seen here in German hands (*L Rogers*)

Capt George Lawrence Lloyd MC AFC. A South African, 'Zulu' Lloyd flew with the unit from April 1917. He scored four victories with No 60 Sqn until mid-July, when he was transferred to No 40 Sqn as a Flight commander, where an additional four victories brought his total to ten

artillery officers, who took me off to their mess and offered me a "tot", which was thankfully received, while they sent off a message to the squadron. The following is the official list of damage done to my machine. Six bullet holes in the propeller. Cowling shot away. Large holes in bottom of petrol tank and sides. Main spar right hand top plane broken. Rear right hand undercarriage strut badly damaged Twenty-eight holes in fuselage, and ten in the planes, two or three missing the pilot's head by less than an inch.' Molesworth's victor was Offstv K Gregor of *Jasta* 29, who claimed a Nieuport south-west of Fresnoy at 1810 hrs. Molesworth was credited with an Albatros destroyed from the first fight. Lt R G Sillers claimed another, sent down smoking, and Lt W E Jenkins claimed an Albatros out of control east of Lens. 2Lt G 'Zulu' Lloyd also claimed an Albatros destroyed and another out of control, possibly Hptm Adolf von Tutschek who force landed his damaged fighter, shot in the engine.

With the successful conclusion of the Messines offensive the pilots were given a rest of one day in three and took the advantage to let off steam. One pilot recalled, 'Four of us aviated over to Paris-Plage, near Etaples, this afternoon and tested our grids by firing into the sea. Afterwards we landed opposite the Hotel Continental and left our machines there under guard. We wandered about the village for a bit and then started for home, stunting about to amuse the populace, which had collected on the front to see us off. We all got home safely just as it was getting dark.'

During June, the weather was extremely hot. Molesworth wrote, 'The only ways of keeping cool are flying or sitting under the trees in the orchard. We spend most of the day, when not in the air, in multi-coloured pyjamas, some lads even going so far as to fly in them.' Some pilots each dug a hole, about a foot deep and three feet long, and covered it with a ground sheet, pegged down at the corners, making a single-seat bath in which they could lie with a cooling drink and a book, although they took the risk of being bombarded with mud, stones and various other missiles thrown at them by the more energetic and lively spirits in the camp. These single baths were such a success that a large pool, twenty feet square by three feet deep was dug. 'When we got this going the whole population of the nearest village had to come and watch us. This was rather disconcerting, as we used to bathe *tout à fait* nude. Most of the chaps managed to rig up something in the way of a bathing dress by buying various articles of clothing in the neighbouring village, but I was forced to content myself with a type of female undergarment, which seemed to cause great amusement amongst the ack-emmas. The village maidens were highly delighted and thought it quite the thing, now that we were decently clad, to watch us at our aquatic sports.' The three Flight commanders shared a Nissen hut, with 'Saloon Bar' painted in black on one of its windows, but as most of the squadron congregated there – including Kate and Black Boy, two of the squadron's dogs – they renamed it Hotel du Commerce.

July saw more victories. On the 3rd, six Nieuports of B Flight, led by Caldwell, were returning from a patrol in the evening when they attacked seven Albatros scouts near Graincourt, sending one down out of control. Regaining their height, the Flight next attacked five enemy scouts, driving them east. There was a strong westerly wind blowing, the Nieuports were at the end of their endurance, and Caldwell decided to abandon the chase. Returning to the lines, approaching Graincourt again, Caldwell saw three Albatros scouts below and led the Flight down to attack them. Caldwell later wrote: 'when leading a Nieuport Flight over the lines in a strong adverse wind, I dawdled too long, hoping for a quick shot at a Hun formation below us, left it too late, and we lost a fellow named Adam, brought down by a "zooming" Albatros from below. I was naturally very upset at this bad judgement on my part. We had a job extricating the others from a bad situation as I remember.' These 'others' were pilots of C Flight, who were flying top cover for B Flight. They had dived into the fight and Lt F O Soden claimed an Albatros out of control, but Lt Alexander R Adam was wounded, taken POW, later dying of his wounds. He was claimed by Ltn Ballik of *Jasta* 12.

On 7 July, 'Zulu' Lloyd, the South African, scored his fourth victory, an Albatros scout out of control over Wancourt at 1145 hrs. The day also saw a portent of things to come, with Caldwell making his first

Lt Pope and Lt Frank Soden standing in front of a Nieuport (*L Rogers*)

flight in an SE 5. The unit was being re-equipped with the SE 5 and the next day Caldwell flew to No 56 Sqn to discuss the new machines, the squadron having been flying the type since the previous April.

Maj Scott returned from leave on 7 July. He had been told that he would shortly be promoted to command a Wing and, realising that this would curtail his combat flying even further, he decided to make the most of his remaining time by flying as often as possible. Just before 2000 hrs on 10 July, a message was received that British troops in the vicinity of Monchy-le-Preux were being attacked by 12 enemy aircraft. Pilots were playing tennis, but when the Klaxon horn went off, Scott, Bishop, Soden and others ran to their machines. Seven Nieuports reached the area under attack and engaged the enemy machines at 1000 ft, just as they were heading back to their base. Scott flamed a machine, one of two which was attacking Bishop, and the Canadian sent the other down out of control, but in the general fighting Scott was badly wounded and his Nieuport so extensively damaged that it barely got him

Lt Frank Ormond Soden. Soden served with No 60 Sqn from June 1917 until February 1918, scoring 16 victories with the unit. He returned to France in July 1918 as a Flight commander in No 41 Sqn, scoring another 11 victories, bringing his total to 27. He served in the RAF both in the inter-war years and in World War 2. Soden died in 1961

back to Filescamp Farm. Ground crew helped the major out of his machine, blood running down his sleeve and he was rushed to hospital, the third of the unit's commanding officers to be a casualty from enemy action. Scott's replacement was Capt W J C K Cochran-Patrick, MC and Bar and DSO. A Flight commander with 23 Sqn and an ace with 21 victories, he was promoted to major and took command.

For the remainder of the month, while training on the SE 5s, the unit continued to fly patrols in its Nieuports. Despite varying weather conditions there was no shortage of combats or victories. On 11 July, Molesworth, now A Flight commander, claimed an Albatros scout and the following day Bishop crashed an Albatros D III over the Vitry area at 1340 hrs. Frank Soden forced another to land five minutes later, but was attacked by a black Albatros and his machine was so badly damaged that it was later struck off squadron strength. Jenkins destroyed an Albatros scout over Vis-en-Artois at noon the following day. On 15 July, B Flight attacked five Albatros scouts from *Jasta* 12, patrolling with four white-tailed Albatros from *Jasta* 30. Caldwell, Jenkins and W B Sherwood shared in an Albatros D III, which was seen by British troops to crash at Vitry, but Lt G A H Parkes, was shot down and taken prisoner by Oblt Adolf Ritter von Tutschek, Staffelführer of *Jasta* 12. Although wounded in the arm, Parkes put his Nieuport down safely, but was prevented from setting fire to it by von Tutschek, who circled it, firing his guns until troops arrived to take Parkes prisoner. The Nieuport was repaired by the Germans and flown two days later. Returning from this patrol Caldwell, Jenkins and Sherwood shared in

Bishop and Maj Scott at Filescamp Farm, June 1917

Nieuport 23 B1575. Lt G A H Parkes was wounded and taken prisoner flying this Nieuport on 15 July 1917 (*L Rogers*)

2Lt Gerald Hickling Parkes (sitting) in Trier POW camp, December 1917. Parkes was shot down on 15 July 1917 in Nieuport 23 B1575. Parkes was the unit's last Nieuport loss (*M O'Connor*)

another Albatros, which they forced to land at Moeuvres. This was possibly Ltn Erich Schlegelmilch of *Jasta* 29 who was slightly wounded on this date.

Low clouds and rain on 18 July stopped flying for two days, but on the 20th the day was fine and clear. After lunch, Bishop scored his last victory on a Nieuport, sending an Albatros down out of control south east of Havrincourt at 1205 hrs. On 23 July, the unit's pilots claimed their last victory while flying Nieuports, Molesworth, F C Parkes and Penny destroying a balloon over Récourt.

On 28 July, Bishop opened the scoring on the squadron's new SE 5s. Flying SE 5 A8936, he flamed an Albatros over Phalempin at 1810 hrs. The following day, Bishop, Caldwell and Gunner spotted a Aviatik two-seater over Beaumont. They attacked this machine, but it was a decoy for four Albatros scouts of *Jasta* 12, who came down on the British scouts from out of the early morning sun. The engine of

On 22 July 1917 a cameraman visited the unit and shot footage of the pilots and their activities. This famous still from the sequence shows, from left to right, 2Lt Jenkins, Lt Soden, Capt Bishop, Capt Caldwell and Capt Molesworth. Molesworth commented on the occasion, 'Charlie Chaplin isn't in it now with us! We were cinematographed the other day. Some of us stood in a row and tried to look pleasant and unconcerned, but this was rather difficult, as everyone else was making rude remarks about us. We then bundled into our new grids, which we have just got, and started off on a stunt formation, nearly running down the old cinema man to put the wind up him. After we had done a circuit, my radiator began to boil, and I was forced to come down. Thank heaven! it was a good landing, as the old man was still at it turning the handle. My part of the show was to be known as 'Pilot landing for more ammunition after fierce fight.' The new 'grids' referred to by Molesworth were the first SE 5s to be issued to the unit

Gunner's SE 5 began to run badly and he broke off the action and made for the lines, but he was seen by von Tutschek. Caldwell and Bishop both fired at the black Albatros from long range, hoping to force the Staffelführer to break off his attack, but Gunner's SE 5 burst into flames under von Tutschek's fire and it crashed near Henin-Liétard at 2000 hrs for the German's 21st victory and his *Jasta's* 100th. Three additional enemy aircraft had now joined in the fight and Bishop and Caldwell were hard pressed. Bishop sent a scout down out of control and Caldwell fired several bursts at another until both his guns jammed. Two enemy scouts then got onto Caldwell's tail and he was forced down to only 80 ft before he could shake them off. Caldwell had not been able to clear his gun jams, but seeing that Bishop, eight miles over the lines, was in trouble with other enemy scouts, Caldwell climbed back into the fight. Although he had no operative guns, Caldwell's presence caused the enemy pilots to break off the action and he and Bishop returned to base, landing just before a violent storm broke. Bad weather kept the unit on the ground for the last two days of the month.

Disciplinary Sgt Maj J A Aspinall, standing by the propeller of an SE5, was one of the outstanding characters in the unit. Sgt A A Nicod said of him: 'He was a fine soldier and possibly the principal humorist of the Squadron, although the humour was often unconscious. He was called with all reverence 'The Great Man' by the officers and generally 'Jimmy' by the rank and file

THIRD YPRES

The next Allied offensive in Flanders was scheduled to begin on 28 July and air preparations had begun on the 8th. The weather was extremely bad on the initial starting date, and the offensive was postponed until 31 July, when the attack opened on a front stretching from the Lys valley in the south to Jansboek in the north, the troops moving out of their trenches at 0530 hrs. Despite the continuing rain, attacks on German aerodromes were made by fighter aircraft of the Army Wings and contact patrols were flown, with six aircraft lost, three personnel killed, ten wounded and three taken as POW.

In August, the bad weather continued, with heavy rain for the first three days of the month, making flying impossible. Conditions had improved by the evening of 5 August. A patrol led by Capt Molesworth attacked enemy aircraft over Hendecourt, and Molesworth and Horn flamed an Albatros D III, killing Ltn Lehmann of *Jasta* 12. Bishop also claimed an Albatros in flames at the same time and area 'near' two SE 5s, but Lehmann was the only German casualty of the day and Bishop's claim, although allowed, was clearly one of 'poaching'. Bishop claimed another Albatros the next day, at 1545 hrs over Brebieres, but again there are no recorded German losses. On 9 August, Molesworth and Horn attacked enemy machines at 0700 hrs over Cagnicourt. Molesworth crashed a scout and Horn claimed another driven down out of control. Two hours later Bishop claimed an Albatros two-seater, crashed at Ecourt.

Although the serial number is not shown, photographic evidence points to the possibility that this is SE 5 A4853, which was allocated to the unit from No 56 Sqn, where it had been flown by Lt C Lewis and Lt D S Wilkinson. Painted red in No 56 Sqn, in No 60 Sqn the headrest was probably repainted blue, the Flight colour. In August 1917, No 60 Sqn had 14 SE 5s on squadron strength and one SE 5a. Flight markings of coloured engine cowlings, lower wing root fairings, footstep, bottom of rudder and a diagonal band around the rear of the fuselage, all outlined in white. These markings were in red for A Flight, yellow for B Flight, with C Flight in blue. These colourful markings were not approved by Wing, and on 26 August they were replaced by Flight letters and a squadron marking of a white disc on the fuselage behind the roundel, repeated on the top decking of the fuselage

On 11 August, conditions were cloudy, no flying was scheduled and the unit celebrated the award of Bishop's VC. J Warne, the squadron's historian recorded, 'It was a wonder the whole place did not go up in flames. Brig Gen Higgins, GOC III Brigade, was thrown out of a Mess window, but he returned to give someone else the same treatment; uniforms were ripped apart; the piano got its fair share of champagne, as usual, and even the rats were distraught by the noise and hubbub, taking shelter in the unoccupied huts of the unsuspecting revellers.'

On 13 August, Bishop claimed two Albatros scouts in flames – one painted with silver 'fish' scales – five miles south of Douai at 1902 hrs. Despite these positive claims, the *Jagdstaffeln* reported no casualties. Two days later A Flight – Molesworth, Pope, H Hammond and Alexander Beck – destroyed a balloon and Molesworth destroyed another for his ninth and final victory with the unit. He was posted back to HE and temporary command of A Flight was given to Spenser Horn before eventually going to Capt Leslie Chidlaw-Roberts, who joined the squadron on 18 August.

On 17 August, William Bishop left for HE. In five months he had claimed 47 enemy aircraft and two balloons. Warne, commenting on the Canadian's victories and departure, wrote: 'many were claimed on solo sorties over the other side of the Lines and not substantiated for that reason.'

William Earle Molesworth had also now come to the end of his tour. 'This morning the CO sent for me to go to the orderly room. He told me that my time had come through for HE and congratulated me on having been awarded the MC. Later I went round to the sheds to say goodbye to the men and finally ended up in the Mess to have a farewell drink with all my old friends. I can hardly realise that the time has

Bishop's SE 5 A8936 on No 3 Sqn's aerodrome at Lechelle, July 1917 (*L Rogers*)

Capt Bishop, Capt Molesworth and 2Lt Young in front of the Saloon Bar, Hotel du Commerce, at Filescamp Farm in summer 1917 (*L Rogers*)

come for me to go back to Blighty ... I can't help feeling sad at leaving this dear old place – full of memories, sometimes tragic, sometimes comic. It's very hard to part with these comrades of mine – "Knights of the Air" – who live from day to day facing eternity with a smile, and laying down their lives, if need be, with such heroism, for the cause of freedom.'

Spenser 'Nigger' Horn scored the last victory claimed in August, with a two-seater, over Gillemont Farm at 1715 hrs on the 26th. This machine, from *Fl Abt (A)* 210, crewed by Ltn d R Brandenberger and Ltn Sanger was seen to fall in flames by British anti-aircraft batteries.

In France the rainfall in July and August 1917 had been the worst for over 75 years and the first days of September saw little improvement. On 4 September, C Flight, led by Horn, forced an Albatros two-seater to land and the following day Horn and J B Crompton sent an Albatros scout down out of control over Sailly-en-Ostrevent for the last victory to be scored by the squadron while at Filescamp Farm.

On 7 September, the unit was transferred to 11th Wing, now under the command of its old commanding officer, Alan Scott, now a Lt Col, and moved north to Ste-Marie-Cappel, east of St Omer. The pilots were unhappy at having to leave the comfortable accommodation and facilities that had been built up over the nine months at Filescamp Farm, and although Nissen huts were eventually erected to replace the dug-in bell tents, living conditions never approached those of Filescamp Farm. These annoyances were also exacerbated by the small size of the landing area, resulting in landing accidents.

THIRD YPRES – THE BATTLE FOR THE MENIN ROAD RIDGE

The unit was now operating on the 2nd and 5th Army fronts. The offensive was to begin on 20 September, and in addition to their defence of the Corps squadrons' two-seaters working over the lines, the 12 fighter squadrons of II Brigade, V Brigade and 9th Wing were to carry out extensive ground strafing of enemy troops and positions, aerodromes and assembly points. In preparation for this work, the squadron's machines – nine SE 5s and nine SE 5as – were fitted with racks to carry four 25 lb Cooper fragmentation anti-personnel bombs.

The first patrols from the new base were flown on 11 September, Lt Jack Rutherford damaging a two-seater over Polygon Wood. The next day, Chidlaw-Roberts led A Flight on a Northern OP, from Westroosbeke to Gheluwe, with Caldwell leading B Flight on a Southern OP from Quesnoy. After dropping their bombs in the trenches, both Flights were involved in a fight with enemy scouts over Menin and during the fighting Henry 'Bunny' Hammond was shot down. Having trouble with his engine, and with both guns jammed, Hammond had left the fight and made for the front line, but was attacked by two Albatros. Hit by their fire, the Australian force landed in the German trenches near La Bassée and was taken prisoner. The pilots of A Flight were awarded an Albatros out of control from the fight. On 16 September, an early evening Northern patrol by A Flight saw a great deal of fighting over Houthem. Ltn Alfred Bauer of *Jasta* 17 was killed, his Albatros seen to crash in No-Man's-Land by British anti-aircraft batteries. Bauer was awarded to Chidlaw-Roberts for his second victory. Lt H A Hamersley shot the wings off another Albatros which was seen going down out of control and Pope sent one down with smoke coming from its engine. Offsetting these losses, South African Lt John Hawtrey was wounded,

Capt William James Rutherford. A Canadian from Montreal, 'Jack' Rutherford was posted to the unit in April 1917. In October he was promoted to captain and given command of C Flight. He scored eight victories before returning to HE in December 1917 and eventually to Canada in 1918

Lt H T Hammond in SE 5a A8918 was forced to land by ground fire on 14 September 1917

Early morning, Ste-Marie-Cappel, September 1917. 'Grid' Caldwell relaxing in his tent

shot down and taken POW by Ltn Fitzner of *Jasta* 17, dying of his wounds the following day.

On 20 September, during the first hours of the offensive, the unit flew overlapping northern OPs. Starting at 0900 hrs, four machines took off at intervals of 1¼ hrs, the last patrol leaving at 1745 hrs. At 0603 hrs, Bancroft and Lt James Whiting left to bomb the enemy aerodromes at Marke and Bisseghem. Whiting had engine trouble and force landed. Bancroft returned after 37 minutes having encountered heavy mist at 200 ft. He took off again at 0855 hrs, but was forced to land east of Zonnebecke at 0950 hrs by Ltn Hans Adam of *Jasta* 6. Bancroft, who was taken prisoner, was Adam's second victory of the day. At 1030 hrs a patrol led by Frank Soden, with G F Elliot, R B Steele and James Law, the son of Chancellor Arthur Bonar Law, were in combat with eight enemy scouts at 1110 hrs north-east of Zonnebecke. Soden slightly wounded Ltn Löwenhardt of *Jasta* 10 who crash landed from 1500 ft. Soden then had trouble with his guns and landed at No 1 Sqn RNAS aerodrome at Bailleul before returning to

Ste-Marie-Cappel. Law returned to base with his SE 5 badly damaged, but claimed an Albatros from the action. Before the fight, Steele had suffered engine failure, crash landing west of Zonnebecke at 1040 hrs. He was taken to hospital with concussion and facial injuries and struck off strength. In a patrol at noon, 2Lt John Crompton scored his second victory, a two-seater out of control over the Roulers/Menin area at 1245 hrs. Fifteen minutes later he destroyed a balloon over Moorslede. Jack Rutherford was also in the area and destroyed a balloon over Roulers at 1300 hrs. Another patrol led by Soden took off at 1620 hrs. Twenty enemy aircraft were seen. In a fight with six Albatros, Jenkins and Elliott, with Canadian Ian Macgregor, a new arrival, shot down one painted black with grey stripes. Law claimed another out of control, but his SE 5a was badly shot about and he ran out of petrol, force landing just short of the aerodrome.

This intense fighting continued the next day. Chidlaw-Roberts led H A Hamersley, J O Whiting, Ian Macgregor and Law on a OP at 0855 hrs. Chidlaw-Roberts dropped out with a badly leaking radiator, but the others carried on and engaged eight enemy scouts east of Ypres. In the fighting, James Law was shot down and killed by Vfw Schneidewind of *Jasta* 17 for his third victory. Patrols later in the day had better luck. In combat over Langemarck at 1815 hrs Chidlaw-Roberts and Whiting crashed a two-seater and, aided by some Spads, Macgregor destroyed an Albatros south-east of Ypres, following this 30 minutes

**Captains all. Left to right:
R L Chidlaw-Roberts, H D Crompton,
J B Crompton, F O Soden.
Ste-Marie-Cappel, autumn 1917**

later with another in the same area. Both were confirmed by British anti-aircraft batteries. With an enemy aircraft claimed out of control over Langemarcke by Soden at 0700 hrs, plus another destroyed by Graham Young over Langemarcke at 1400 hrs, bringing the victories to six, the gain/loss ratio for the day was good, Law being the only casualty. However, 22 September saw two casualties. Six SE 5s took off at 0925 hrs and an hour and 20 minutes later were fighting 11 Albatros from *Jasta* 26 over Zonnebecke. Chidlaw-Roberts and Alan Hamersley attacked a green and black Albatros sending it down out of control. Vfw Fritz Kosmahl of the *Jasta* survived the crash but died of his wounds four days later. During the fighting, Whiting was shot down by Staffelführer Oblt Bruno Loerzer for his ninth victory and Macgregor, wounded in the leg, was forced to land. There was another casualty the next day. Flying his first patrol since joining the squadron two days before, 2AM Horatio Bright was shot down, killed by Gefr Wirth and Uffz Noerthen, a crew from *Schusta* 10. Bright had previously served as a pilot with Nos 6 and 1 Sqns, but had lost his commission as the result of a court martial while in England.

During the day, elements of A and B Flights, led by Caldwell, saw the beginning of a combat which was to become famous in the annals of aerial combat. Returning from patrol and keeping a watchful eye on over 20 Albatros scouts at 15,000 ft, Hamersley saw what he took to be a Nieuport, with an Albatros on its tail, pass in front of the SE 5as. Hamersley attacked the Albatros but was surprised to see the 'Nieuport' turn towards him and he realised that it was one of the new Fokker Triplanes. Ltn Werner Voss of *Jasta* 10, the pilot of the Fokker, easily outmanoeuvred Hamersley and severely damaged his machine with an accurate burst of fire. Hamersley managed to land the badly damaged

Off Duty. Lt Young being force fed by Armstrong, McCall, Rutherford and Soden. Burk-sur-Mer, August 1917 (*L Rogers*)

Chidlaw-Roberts (left) and Caldwell carry out morning ablutions at Ste-Marie-Cappel, September 1917

On the far right is Robert Chidlaw-Roberts, intent on reading his mail from home. The officer wearing the cap is Kennedy-Cochran-Patrick. In profile nearest the camera is Keith Caldwell

SE 5as of B Flight. Ste-Marie-Cappel, September 1917 (*L Rogers*)

SE 5a at No 29 Sqn's aerodrome, but it was struck off strength. Chidlaw-Roberts had attempted to draw Voss away from Hamersley, but the German ace barely paused in his pursuit. 'In seconds he was on my tail and had shot my rudder bar. I retired from the fray and that was all I saw of it.' Caldwell had seen Hamersley fighting the triplane, but B Flight of No 56 Sqn had now arrived, led by Capt James McCudden, and Caldwell recalled: 'I decided to leave them to it, as 56 were well in command of this one sided scrap.' After a fight against six pilots of No 56 Sqn, lasting ten minutes, Voss was finally shot down and killed by Lt Arthur Rhys Davids.

Patrols on 25 September saw three more victories. At noon, J Crompton and Graham Young crashed an Albatros scout over

On 5 October 1917 2Lt J J Fitzgerald was forced to land SE 5a B507 with engine failure on or near the base of *Jasta* 18 at Harlebeke (*L Rogers*)

SE 5a B507. No longer an object of curiosity to the pilots and ground crew of *Jasta* 18, 2Lt Fitzgerald's SE 5a stands unattended at Harlebecke.

Goenburg, and in an afternoon patrol William Jenkins destroyed a brown two-seater a mile east of Ypres at 1540 hrs. Caldwell sent a green two-seater down out of control north-east of St Julien at 1600 hrs for his last victory with the Squadron and the unit's last victory of the month. The last day of September saw three SE 5as wrecked and a pilot killed. John Flynn had returned from a patrol when his machine suddenly nose dived onto the aerodrome and burst into flames. Exploding ammunition prevented rescuers from pulling Flynn from the flames and he was burnt to death. The undercarriage of Fitzgerald's SE collapsed on landing, and Soden crashed his SE at Dickiebusch after an engine failure.

Grid Caldwell (left) packed and ready to leave on the morning of 12 October 1917. Next to Caldwell are Lt Jenkins and Capt Frederick Selous, the new commander of B Flight. On leaving, Caldwell gave his gramophone and records to his groundcrew

The first two days of October were fine and sunny, but deteriorated as the month went on. The weather was bad for flying on 4 October, with heavy rain, clouds no higher than 400 ft and high winds. On 5 October, despite the still appalling weather, which would continue for some days, the unit flew OPs where possible, and on one, 2Lt J J Fitzgerald was forced to land by engine failure at Harlebeke, the base of *Jasta* 18, and was taken prisoner.

The next victories came on 12 October, when J Crompton crashed an Albatros scout over De Ruite at 0915 hrs and W B Sherwood drove down a DFW two-seater over Moorslede at 1120 hrs.

During the day, Keith Logan 'Grid' Caldwell left the Squadron. Caldwell had served continually in France since 19 July 1916, first with No 8 Sqn, where he claimed one victory, before joining No 60 Sqn on 18 December. In 11 months with the unit, with only a short break of ten weeks on sick leave, he had commanded both C and B Flights, had scored eight victories and had been awarded an MC. The citation read:

'For conspicuous gallantry and devotion to duty when leading offensive patrols. He has personally destroyed five hostile machines and had over 50 contests in the air, in all of which he has displayed splendid skill and fearlessness, and has set an excellent example to his squadron.'

The unit was still experiencing difficulties with the reliability of its SE 5as. Hamersley commented, 'The first geared engines were Wolseleys, with 2000/1170 reduction and a four bladed propeller which gave us little trouble, but later the French engines with the 2000/1500 gears really did go crock on us.' Sgt Maj Nicod commented: 'We experienced a devastating period of bad luck. Pilots would return from a patrol blinded with oil, petrol pipes leaking, dud oil pressure, leaking radiators, choked carburettors, broken gears, or half a propeller through faulty CC gear. Sometimes there was no propeller at all due to gears seizing up, fusing and burning the propeller bosses, and also due to the bosses working loose through faulty grinding of the shaft. This deplorable state existed for some time and seriously retarded the work of the Squadron in spite of super-human efforts to rectify the troubles. The sound of gears, aggravated by faulty carburettors created a noise that would have discouraged any aspirants for flying honours.' Hamersley later recalled: 'Owing to the number of rubber joints in the oiling system and the castor oil used, the latter got so thin when hot that the joints always succeeded in leaking oil, with the result that we lost a number of engines through running out of oil before petrol. I very frequently landed at squadrons nearer the line than Ste-Marie-Capelle to top up with oil on the way home from a patrol.'

On 15 October both Hamersley and Lt G F Court force landed, wrecking their machines. Soden was up for a 'joyride' on 20 October when he saw a British balloon, which had broken free of its moorings, drifting east at 12,000 ft. First making sure there were no observers in the basket, Soden fired at the runaway, which deflated and settled down into a field, where it was surrounded by French and Portuguese troops. Soden landed and persuaded the troops to carry it to a nearby road, intending that it should be picked up by the squadron transport and its fabric used to line the pilots' huts. He was too optimistic: Wing insisted that the balloon be returned to its rightful owners.

During this time Capt Spenser Horn MC, the C Flight commander, left for HE and although he was nearing the end of his tour, the Canadian William 'Jack' Rutherford took command of the Flight. Rutherford had scored only three victories since joining the unit on 25 June, but had taken part in many patrols and ground strafing activities. He would add another five victories before being posted to HE in early November.

On 21 October, Hamersley engaged two Albatros scouts, possibly from *Jasta* 33, which were attacking an RE 8 over Poelcapelle. He sent one down out of control at 1305 hrs and destroyed another ten minutes later in the same area. In an afternoon patrol by C Flight, Rutherford, Soden and Young shared in a two-seater crashed near Houthulst at 1615 hrs. The changeable weather now kept the unit on the ground for the next five days, but on 27 October the weather was fine and two Flights took off at 1250 hrs. Over Bellewarde the patrol was jumped by *Jasta* 3. In the attacking dive, Vfw Carl Menckhoff opened fire at long range, hitting William Sherwood's SE, which burst into flames and crashed between Moorslede and Dadizele. The unit's bad luck continued the next day, with two more casualties. At 0930 hrs, in the vicinity of Westroosbeke, C Flight was in combat with a number of Albatros. Rutherford sent one down out of control over the village and saw another spinning down, but Capt C J Temperley, flying his first patrol with the unit, was wounded in the foot and force landed south west of Vlamertinghe. Ten minutes after extricating themselves from the enemy scouts, Capt C J A Caunter was killed by ground fire. As no one else made a claim, Caunter was awarded the Albatros seen going

down by Rutherford. Chidlaw-Roberts and A Flight were also in action during the morning and engaged a large formation of 30 enemy scouts. Chidlaw-Roberts attacked two of these, but they were exceptional pilots and he was forced down to 4000 ft before they left him and made off east. On 30 October Capt F H B Selous rounded off the victory claims for the month with a two-seater out of control over Moorslede at 1000 hrs.

K L Caldwell, S B Horn, R L Roberts and F H B Selous photographed in October 1917

November was to be a better month. Eighteen victories were claimed for no loss. Despite the unit's tireless mechanics solving many of the engine troubles, there were still forced landings, some with consequent loss of aircraft.

The first day of November was a day of low clouds, mist and rain. Despite these adverse conditions the unit flew patrols in the afternoon. At 1345 hrs over Moorslede, Rutherford and Soden fought an Albatros two-seater and sent it down out of control. Twenty-five minutes later they caught another over the same area and claimed it as out of control. Graham Young was also out and shot down an Albatros scout over Houthulst at 1430 hrs. In a morning patrol on 5 November, six Albatros scouts were attacked over Westroosebeke. Harold Hamersley attacked one which had a bright yellow fuselage and it crashed into a wood a mile north of the town at 1210 hrs. Five minutes later, Frank Soden destroyed another Albatros over Houthulst for his ninth victory. Two more victories were claimed the next day: Rutherford and Soden destroyed a two-seater over Zonnebecke at 0730 hrs, possibly a machine

Capt Robert Leslie Chidlaw-Roberts. Chidlaw-Roberts joined the RFC in May 1915 and flew for six months as an observer with No 2 Sqn. After pilot training he served with No 18 Sqn flying FE 2bs. Posted to No 60 Sqn in August 1917, he flew SE 5as with the unit until January 1918, scoring nine victories and winning an MC. After a rest period in England, he returned to France in the summer of 1918 as a Flight commander in No 40 Sqn, scoring one more victory. He died in June 1989

from *Schusta* 19. William Duncan, who had lost touch with the patrol in the clouds, was over Polygon Wood when he saw a DFW below him. He went down to attack this two-seater, crewed by Vfw Wirtz and Flg Zink of *Schusta* 13, but an accurate burst from Zink's gun hit his SE 5 in the oil pump. Despite this, Duncan forced the DFW down and it was seen to crash a mile north east of Polygon Wood by pilots of No 1 Sqn. Duncan attempted to fly back to base but his oil-starved engine finally seized up and he was forced to land in a ploughed field. This DFW was Duncan's first victory of an eventual 11. Ironically, Wirtz and Zink both survived the crash and claimed Duncan as a victory.

8 November was fine and there was a great deal of fighting in the air. The unit had a highly successful day. Frederick Selous attacked a Rumpler from *Fl Abt (A)* 202, crewed by Vfw Willibald Steinicke and Ltn Horst Brassel and shot its wings off. The stricken machine

In the autumn of 1917, an unidentified photographer in the unit seemed to take delight in photographing his fellow pilots while they were shaving. Left to right: S L G 'Poppy' Pope, also known as 'the Cardinal', G C 'Old' Young (shaving) and Chidlaw-Roberts

crashed near Klein Zillebecke and Steinicke and Brassel were buried by troops of the 8th Battalion South Lancashire Regt. In the afternoon, Chidlaw-Roberts having left on leave, Pope took out A Flight. He first shot down a two-seater over Gheluwe at 1540 hrs, then followed this with another over Ypres. Both victories were confirmed by ground observers. Hamersley, Rutherford and J D McCall were also out, fighting with Albatros scouts of *Jasta* Boelcke over Westroosebeke. Hamersley sent his opponent down to crash at 1540 hrs and Rutherford drove another down out of control, but Jim McCall's SE was badly damaged by Vfw Paul Baeumer. He crash landed 500 yards west of Poelcapelle, but was unhurt.

On 10 November the last of the bloody battles of Passchendaele opened, the troops attacking in heavy rain. Low clouds and rain kept flying to a minimum the next day, but Pope destroyed an Albatros over Gheluwe at 1510 hrs and W E Jenkins flamed a balloon over Ypres

Chidlaw-Roberts and Pope disguised as Russians. By a strange twist of fate, Chidlaw-Roberts was to fly in Russia in 1919

20 minutes later. The weather remained changeable, with low cloud, mist and rain and no further victory claims were made until 18 November, Chidlaw-Roberts and Hamersley destroying a DFW north-west of Westroosebeke at 1145 hrs. Pope had also attacked the DFW but fire from the enemy observer had shattered his propeller and he crash landed in a water-filled mine crater near St Julien, claimed by Ltn Ziegler and Ostv Sattler of *Fl Abt* 45. Pope was pulled out of the water by Canadian troops, taken to a nearby pill box, which was being used as a battalion HQ, and given a mug full of rum, which he promptly drank. Not surprisingly, he then passed out. It was 24 hours before Pope telephoned the squadron to tell them he had survived the crash and he finally arrived back with his arms full of champagne. However, he had a slight leg wound, was taken to hospital in Rouen, then sent back to England.

On 19 November, W Jenkins and W J A Duncan claimed a DFW out of control at 1520 hrs south of Beselare. Twenty five minutes later, aided by Spads of No 23 Sqn, they destroyed an Albatros C type south east of Passchendaele.

CAMBRAI

His resources having been squandered in the Ypres battles – the British dead and missing numbered 80,000 men – Haig now decided to mount a limited local offensive against Cambrai. The effectiveness of ground strafing by low flying aircraft during the Ypres battles, plus the attacks on enemy aerodromes, had been realised and the same tasks were set for the fighter squadrons in the coming offensive. The Cambrai battle was to the south of No 60 Sqn's area, the unit took no part in the operations, and it was not until 23 November that Chidlaw-Roberts scored the unit's last victory of the month, an Albatros scout crashed west of Dadizeele at 1010 hrs. There were two casualties during the day. Returning from a patrol, two B Flight pilots, William Jenkins and Maurice West-Thompson were practising formation flying when they collided and crashed near Poperinghe. Both were killed.

The unit lost another Flight commander on 4 December when Jack Rutherford came to the end of his tour and was posted back to England, along with fellow Canadian James McCall. Rutherford had scored seven victories with the unit and won an MC. Frank Soden was given command of the Flight.

During the summer, twin-engined Gotha bombers from the German *Boghol* units had been attacking targets in the Ypres area and on 11 December No 60 Sqn had their first brush with the large bombers. In the afternoon, flying a solo patrol, Chidlaw-Roberts saw a formation of Gothas heading north-east from Langemarck. He repeatedly attacked these, until they were well east of the lines, and he had exhausted his ammunition. Chidlaw-Roberts had failed to bring one down, but he was awarded an MC for this action, one of considerable bravery.

The weather was now generally bad for war flying and the unit was rested for a week. It resumed operations on 18 December, Soden leading a morning patrol. Three Albatros two-seaters were seen over Gheluvelt at 0815 hrs and Soden and Australian Alan Morey attacked them. Morey hit the observer in one, which went down out of control, but the observer's return fire had hit his SE in the petrol tank and he force landed near Gheluvelt. Soden's guns had jammed in his attack on another of the two-seaters, which went down in a steep dive. Soden had turned for home, flying at only 50 ft, at nearly 160 mph, when his propeller, which had been hit by a burst from the enemy observer, suddenly burst. Soden attempted to put the SE 5 down in a ploughed field, but in trying to avoid some telegraph wires he hit a post. The SE turned two cartwheels, finally stopping upside down, totally wrecked. Soden was unhurt and was flying another patrol two and a half hours later. There was another casualty on 23 December: Canadian 2Lt Ward McLennen was killed in an accident when his SE 5 spun in and burst into flames. His replacement was 2Lt Cyril Ball, brother of Albert Ball. Selous claimed the last victory of the year on 28 December, destroying a Rumpler west of Roulers at 1045 hrs.

On 29 December, Major Cochran-Patrick was posted to England to take a training post. He was replaced as commanding officer of the unit by an Australian, Major Barry Moore.

By the end of December the squadron was firmly settled in at Ste-Marie-Cappel. Shortly after the move there, at the beginning of September, in preparation for the coming winter, Chinese workmen, in their blue padded uniforms, had laid wooden slat walks between all the huts, the Mess, hangars and buildings, and sandbagged all the huts for bomb protection. For entertainment a Church Army hut showed movies every night. One new pilot wrote home: 'We had several good films last night, it hardly seems like war yet.' Like all RFC squadrons, the unit had many pets: 'The squadron boasts sixteen canines at present. The officers' mess possesses five. We are very proud of them. Besides these we have six pigs and twenty five hens. There is no shortage of eggs about the mess. To add to the comfort of the mess we have a fairly good piano and a gramophone. Every time anyone goes on leave he brings back a few records and the collection is now quite large.' People kept warm by various means of exercise, but mainly by playing rugby. Tenders were regularly sent into St Omer for provisions and the squadron ate well. A typical dinner consisted of soup, toast, grilled sole with mustard sauce, sweet, biscuits, cheese and coffee. After dinner, cards and chess were played, or there was music by the squadron band. The majority of the pilots went to bed 'fairly early'.

December 1917 saw the end of 19 months of war flying by No 60 Sqn. The unit had claimed nearly 300 victories but the cost had been high. Twenty eight pilots had been killed in action; eight had been wounded; ten had been taken POW; eight wounded and taken POW; six had been wounded, taken POW and died of their wounds, and three had been killed in flying accidents.

This view of Vickers built SE 5a B507 shows the type of squadron and Flight markings used in late 1917 (*L Rogers*)

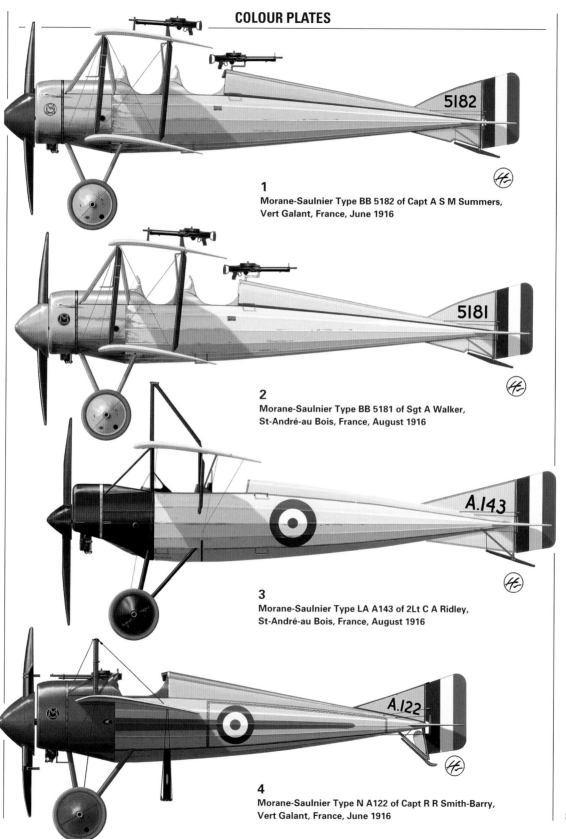

1
Morane-Saulnier Type BB 5182 of Capt A S M Summers,
Vert Galant, France, June 1916

2
Morane-Saulnier Type BB 5181 of Sgt A Walker,
St-André-au Bois, France, August 1916

3
Morane-Saulnier Type LA A143 of 2Lt C A Ridley,
St-André-au Bois, France, August 1916

4
Morane-Saulnier Type N A122 of Capt R R Smith-Barry,
Vert Galant, France, June 1916

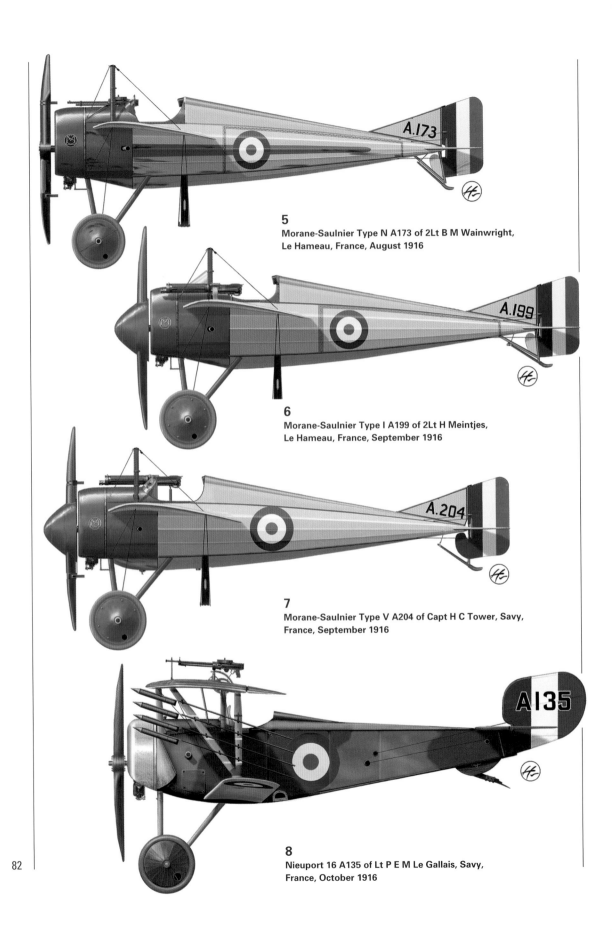

5
Morane-Saulnier Type N A173 of 2Lt B M Wainwright,
Le Hameau, France, August 1916

6
Morane-Saulnier Type I A199 of 2Lt H Meintjes,
Le Hameau, France, September 1916

7
Morane-Saulnier Type V A204 of Capt H C Tower, Savy,
France, September 1916

8
Nieuport 16 A135 of Lt P E M Le Gallais, Savy,
France, October 1916

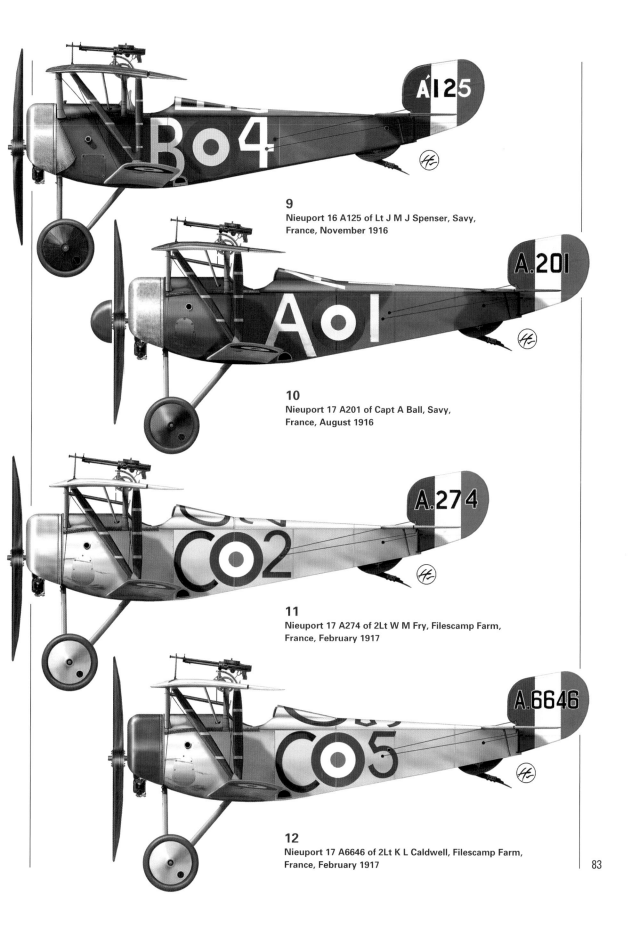

9
Nieuport 16 A125 of Lt J M J Spenser, Savy,
France, November 1916

10
Nieuport 17 A201 of Capt A Ball, Savy,
France, August 1916

11
Nieuport 17 A274 of 2Lt W M Fry, Filescamp Farm,
France, February 1917

12
Nieuport 17 A6646 of 2Lt K L Caldwell, Filescamp Farm,
France, February 1917

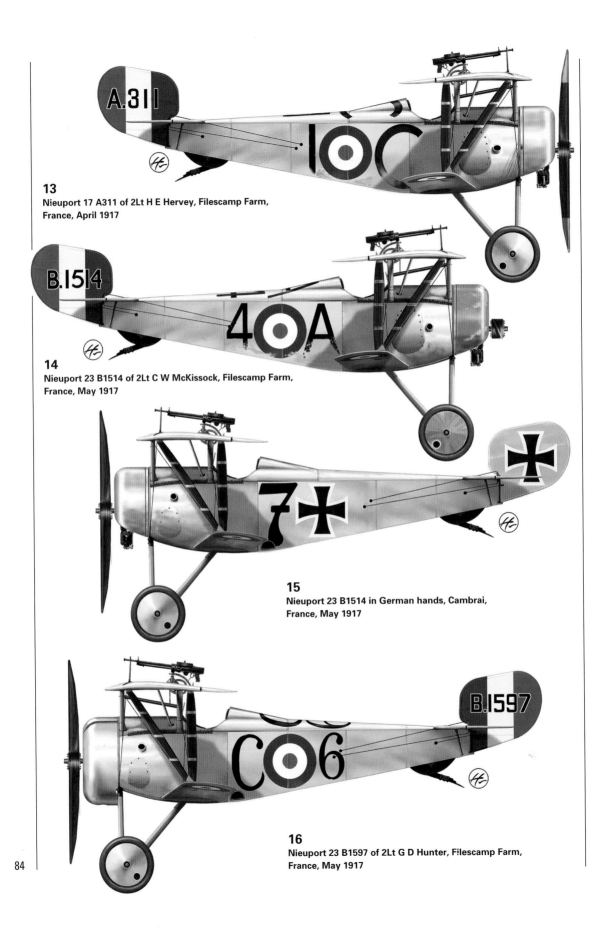

13
Nieuport 17 A311 of 2Lt H E Hervey, Filescamp Farm,
France, April 1917

14
Nieuport 23 B1514 of 2Lt C W McKissock, Filescamp Farm,
France, May 1917

15
Nieuport 23 B1514 in German hands, Cambrai,
France, May 1917

16
Nieuport 23 B1597 of 2Lt G D Hunter, Filescamp Farm,
France, May 1917

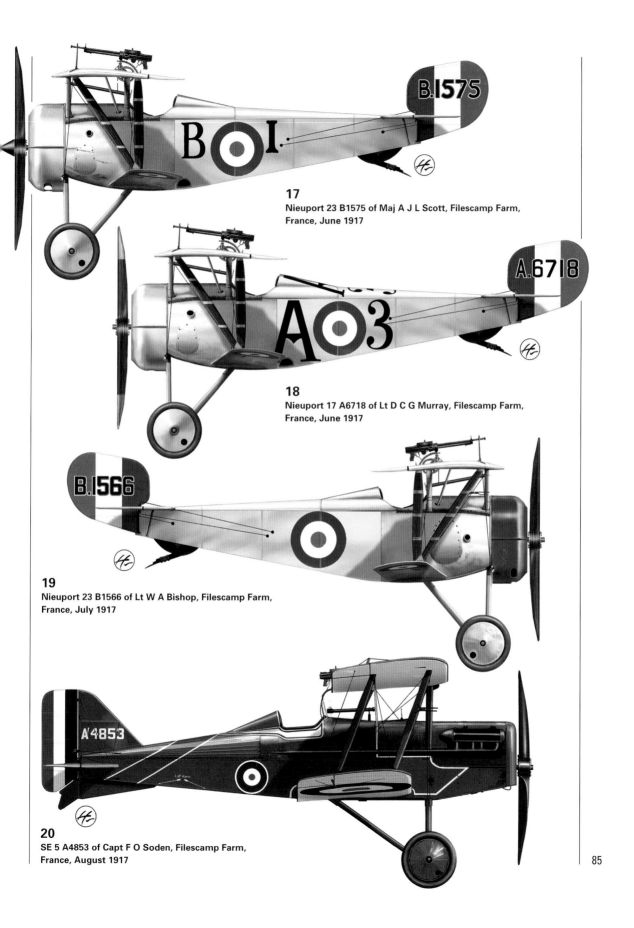

17
Nieuport 23 B1575 of Maj A J L Scott, Filescamp Farm,
France, June 1917

18
Nieuport 17 A6718 of Lt D C G Murray, Filescamp Farm,
France, June 1917

19
Nieuport 23 B1566 of Lt W A Bishop, Filescamp Farm,
France, July 1917

20
SE 5 A4853 of Capt F O Soden, Filescamp Farm,
France, August 1917

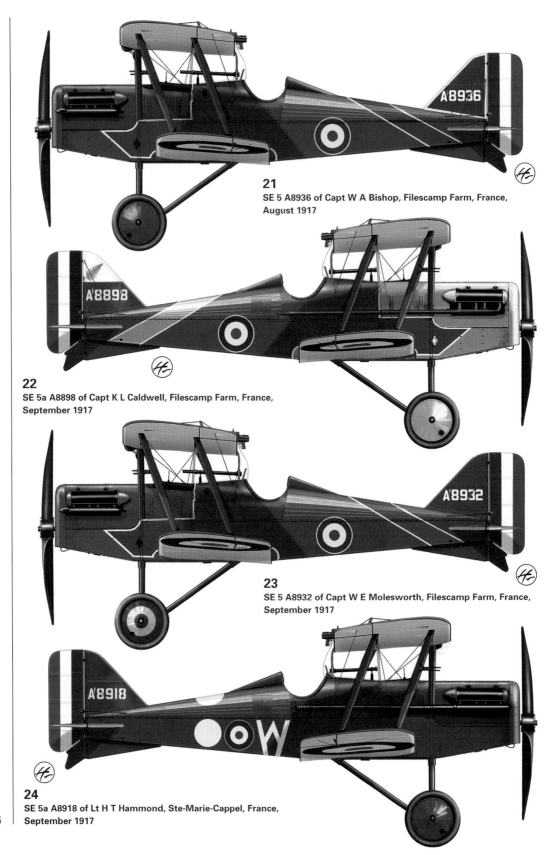

21
SE 5 A8936 of Capt W A Bishop, Filescamp Farm, France,
August 1917

22
SE 5a A8898 of Capt K L Caldwell, Filescamp Farm, France,
September 1917

23
SE 5 A8932 of Capt W E Molesworth, Filescamp Farm, France,
September 1917

24
SE 5a A8918 of Lt H T Hammond, Ste-Marie-Cappel, France,
September 1917

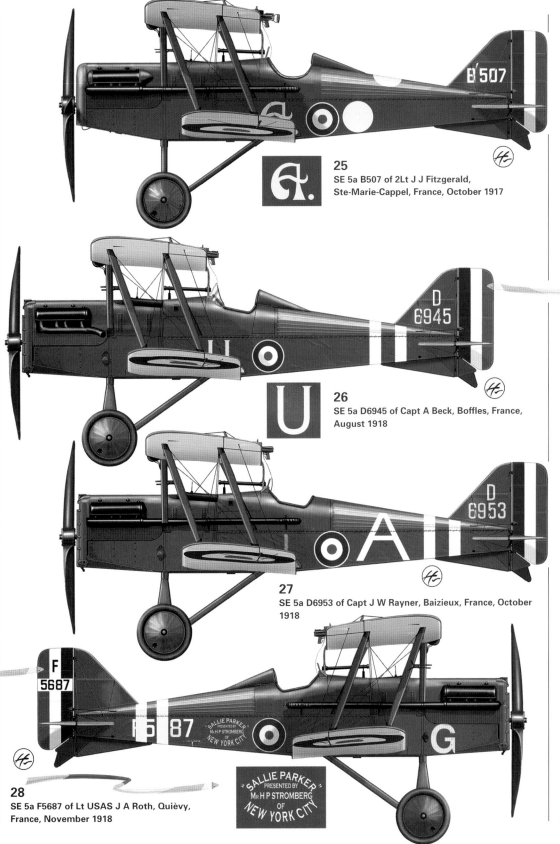

25
SE 5a B507 of 2Lt J J Fitzgerald,
Ste-Marie-Cappel, France, October 1917

26
SE 5a D6945 of Capt A Beck, Boffles, France,
August 1918

27
SE 5a D6953 of Capt J W Rayner, Baizieux, France, October
1918

28
SE 5a F5687 of Lt USAS J A Roth, Quièvy,
France, November 1918

"SALLIE PARKER"
PRESENTED BY
Mr H P STROMBERG
OF
NEW YORK CITY

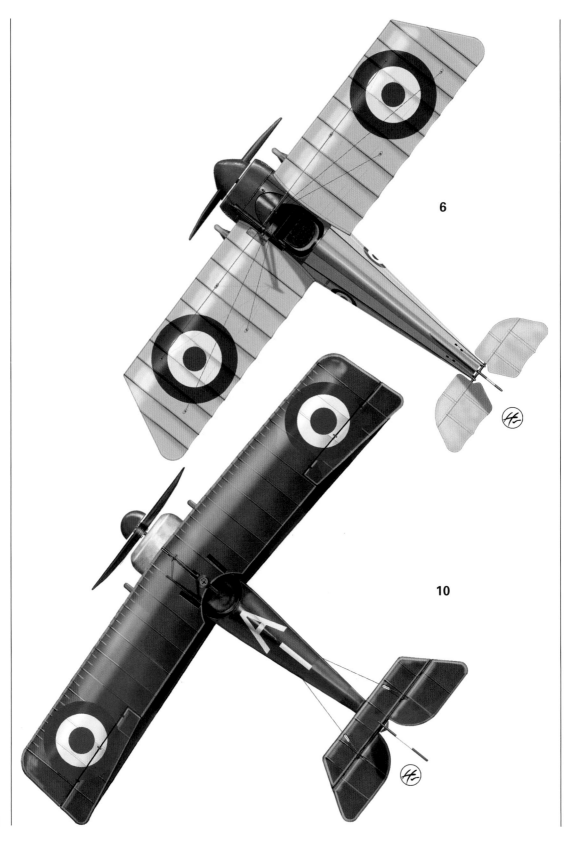

6

10

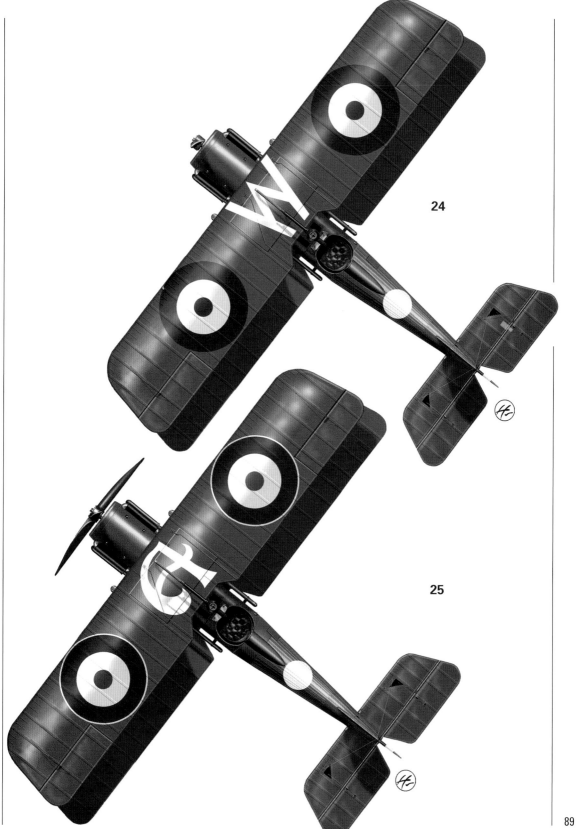

24

25

1918 – MOVES AND ALARMS

New Year's Day saw a great deal of fighting by the fighter squadrons. A patrol from No 60 Sqn joined up with the Spads of No 23 Sqn and the combined force caught a pair of DFW two-seaters working over the lines. Soden and John Crompton shared in sending one down out of control west of Roulers at 1045 hrs. There was little activity the next day, low clouds at 400 ft were heavy with snow and there was a ground mist. The weather cleared on 3 January, a fine, clear day. In an afternoon patrol, Chidlaw-Roberts and C F Cunningham flamed a two-seater over the Comines/Menin area at 1240 hrs, confirmed by British anti-aircraft batteries. A patrol flown in the morning of 4 January saw the unit's first casualty of the new year. Chidlaw-Roberts was leading a patrol of A and B Flights but was forced to return with an overheating engine. Frederick Selous took over command and at 1145 hrs over Menin dived to attack a two-seater several thousand feet below, signalling the remainder of the patrol to stay above for cover. During his dive – estimated by the other pilots to have been in excess of 300 mph – all the wings of Selous's SE 5a C5334 broke away from the fuselage.

There was another loss on 6 January. John Crompton, the new commander of B Flight after the loss of Selous, was leading a patrol in the Menin area when he saw his fellow Canadian 2Lt O Thamer flying northwards at 15,000 ft. Thamer failed to return and it was later found that he had landed in Holland, where he was interned for the remainder of the war, his SE 5a B4885 being impressed into the Dutch Air Service.

The weather was still changeable, with frequent snow showers and the unit was not in action again until 9 January. At 1135 hrs a patrol led by Chidlaw-Roberts joined in a fight over Moorslede between the RE 8s of No 21 Sqn and seven Albatros scouts from *Jasta* Boelcke, led by Ltn Max Müller, the Staffelführer, an ace with 36 victories. An observer in one of the RE 8s, 2Lt Somerville, had fired 50 rounds from very close range at Müller's machine and the German ace broke off his attack. Chidlaw-Roberts and Soden, who had been fighting another four Albatros, now appeared on the scene and fired at Müller as he dived away. Neither British pilot saw the result of this attack, but a report from HQ 11th Wing confirmed that the Albatros went down in flames, with Müller jumping to his death. Although Somerville had forced Müller to dive away, the No 60 Sqn pilots were credited with the victory, probably correctly, as Ltn Baeumer of the *Jasta* reported that Müller had broken off his attack on the British two-seater because of gun jams and was then hit by two SE 5s.

On 14 January the unit was visited by Capt James McCudden. The B Flight commander in No 56 Sqn, McCudden had scored 20 victories

Left Capt Frederick H B Selous.
Selous was killed in action on
4 January 1918 when his SE 5a broke
up in mid-air. Exactly a year to the
day previously, his father, Capt
Frederick Courteney Selous DSO,
famed explorer, big game hunter
and conservationist, was killed by a
German sniper's bullet while fighting
on the banks of the Rufiji River in
South Africa. General von
Lettow-Vorbeck, commander of the
German forces in South Africa, later
sent a personal note of condolence,
apologising for the 'ungentlemanly
death' of Selous

Right Lt Sydney Leo Gregory Pope.
'Poppy' Pope served with the unit
from June to November 1917,
scoring six victories and winning an
MC. Pope was shot down behind the
British lines on 18 November 1917,
returning to the squadron 24 hours
later. In the 1938 film *Dawn Patrol*,
starring Errol Flynn and David Niven,
Niven's character is shot down and
given up for dead, only to return
with bottles of champagne in his
arms. Having seen the film, and
meeting Niven at a party in World
War 2, 'Poppy' Pope delightedly
told him: 'That was me!'

since the previous November – 19 two-seaters and one scout – and on the day before his visit had destroyed three two-seaters in a morning patrol. Impressed by McCudden's tactics in destroying enemy two-seaters, Alan Scott, now a Lt Col in command of 11th Wing, asked McCudden to tour the fighter squadrons under his command, Nos 1, 19 and 60, to lecture on his methods.

The weather continued unfavourable and it was not until 24 January that the next combats, and loss, were recorded. A patrol at noon was attacked by an Albatros, which dived out of the sun and attacked Lt Fred Clark. Alan Morey saw this, turned towards the enemy scout, but collided with it, cutting it in half and losing both wings from one side of his SE at 12,000 ft. The Albatros pilot killed in the collision was Ltn M Möbius who, bizarrely, was awarded Morey as a victory. The next day Hamersley's patrol was in combat with elements of *Jasta* 7 fighting an FE 2b of No 20 Sqn and DH 4s of No 25 Sqn. Hamersley attacked a black Albatros with a letter K on its fuselage, flown by Ltn Kunst of *Jasta* 7 who crash landed near Staden.

Two more victories on 28 January rounded off the month. In an afternoon patrol H G Hegarty and Soden each claimed an Albatros scout out of control – Hegarty at 1320 hrs north of Kortmark and Soden ten minutes later over Handzame.

February began well. Although the aerodrome was bombed on the night of the 3rd no damage was done. On 4 February Lts William Duncan and J O Priestley flamed an Albatros at 1120 hrs over Ypres, killing Ltn Bruno Langer of *Jasta* 3. Five minutes later the Flight attacked a formation of Albatros over Zonnebecke, Lts H Crompton and Hegarty shooting one down in flames. The next day a morning patrol was in action with Albatros of *Jasta* 26. Cyril Ball, the younger brother of Albert Ball, was following an Albatros down when he was attacked by Offstv Esswein, whose fire hit Ball's SE 5 in the engine. Ball was forced to land and was taken prisoner. Frank Soden claimed two Albatros during the morning. His patrol attacked four Albatros near Gheluvelt and Soden sent one down out of control before stoppages in both guns forced him to leave the action. Two enemy scouts then got

Lt H Guy, the unit's Recording Officer, with friend, Ste-Marie-Cappel, September 1917

on his tail as he dived for the safety of the front line, eight miles away. Over Houthulst Forest, down to 50 ft, Soden turned sharply and one of the pursuing Albatros pilots hit a tree and crashed. This was Soden's 16th and last victory while serving with the unit. His posting to HE came through in the evening and bad weather kept him on the ground until he left the squadron on 14 February.

On 9 February, Capt Robert Leslie Chidlaw-Roberts, the A Flight commander, left for Home Establishment. He had served in the unit since August 1917, been awarded nine victories and had won an MC. Capt H D Crompton took over the Flight.

Bad weather curtailed war flying for some days and it was not until 18 February that the unit was next in action. Hamersley, the new C Flight commander, took his pilots into an action with Fokker Triplanes north of Handzame at 1240 hrs, the first of the type seen by the squadron. Hamersley sent one down to crash and Lts C O Evans and R B Clark forced another down to ground level, where it crashed into a tree. The Canadian, Lt W M Kent, claimed another as destroyed. Next day, Morley Kent claimed another victory. Joining in a fight between Albatros scouts and Spads and Camels of Naval 1 and 10 Squadrons, he fired at an Albatros from extreme range – 400 yards. This Albatros, flown by Lt Hans von Puttkammer of *Jasta* 3, went down to crash land in the British lines. Puttkammer was taken POW and his Albatros No 4495/17 was designated G 138. Kent was awarded this as a victory, but it was almost certainly the work of FSL Stanley Rosevere of Naval 1 and Flt Cdr Alfred Carter of Naval 10.

At 0900 hrs on the morning of 21 February, a patrol was in action with Albatros scouts of *Jasta* 27 over Houthulst Forest and Morley Kent was shot down and killed by Ltn Rudolf Klimke. Lt George B Craig, an American masquerading as a Canadian, as did so many of his countrymen in the RFC, was attacked by the Staffelführer, Oblt Hermann Göring. Craig put up a courageous fight, seriously damaging Göring's Albatros, but eventually he was wounded and landed to be taken POW, dying of his wounds the next day. Kent and Craig were both buried in the same grave at Moorsele.

Although the weather was very changeable for the remainder of the month, and there was some air fighting, the unit claimed no additional

At Ste-Marie-Cappel, autumn 1917. Left to right: H D Crompton, R L Chidlaw-Roberts, F O Soden. Sitting is a remarkably young looking Lt F W Clark (*L Rogers*)

victories. March was to start badly. A South African pilot, J C Low, stalled on take-off. He suffered head injuries in the subsequent crash and was taken to hospital. Two days later, returning from an Offensive Patrol, another new pilot, Lt Len Southwell, a native of Bath, crashed at Bailleul and was seriously injured, dying on 14 March.

MOVES, RETREATS AND OFFENSIVES

By the beginning of March it was known that the next German offensive would be against the British Third and Fifth Armies. One third of the attack would be against Third Army in the north, with the remainder of the attacks held by Fifth Army. From the beginning of the month the duty of the RFC squadrons was to report on and interfere with the enemy preparations. In the first days of the month the *Luftstreitkräfte* was relatively inactive, husbanding its strength, for the first time greater than that of the RFC. The duties of the RFC fighter squadrons were Close and Distant Patrols; the Close Patrols in the area from north to south, ten miles east of the front line; the Distant Patrols the same area but extending ten miles further east.

The clouds were very low on 1 March and only a few flights were made. Low clouds, strong winds, mist and snow, then stopped all flying for the next three days and it was not until 5 March that preparations began. As part of these, No 60 Sqn moved to the Town aerodrome, east of Bailleul, on 8 March. The aerodrome was considerably nearer to the front line and came under daily shellfire. The hangars were situated just behind a small graveyard, which was hit by two heavy shells, and pieces of gravestones fell around the hangars and aircraft.

Left to right: 2Lt C G Evans, H D Crompton, J B Crompton (Canadian)

The first patrols from the new base were flown on 9 March. Hamersley, leading C Flight, attacked a slate-coloured Pfalz D III over Menin, which crashed at Dadizeele at 1135 hrs. Captain H D Crompton and William Duncan of A Flight were also successful, each claiming an Albatros out of control over Gheluwe, five and ten minutes later. Crompton's victory was the last he was to claim with the unit. On 15 March he was flying a Wireless Interception Flight when his engine failed. He was injured in the subsequent forced landing and sent to hospital. His replacement as A Flight commander was Capt Walter Copeland. The unit lost another Flight commander two days later when Capt John Bonnicher Crompton was sent to hospital and struck off strength. His replacement was Capt Kelvin Crawford, a former Flight commander with No 24 Sqn, credited with five victories.

The squadron now had a number of new pilots on strength, all needing to be adequately trained before flying on operations. Consequently, although there was a great deal of air fighting over the next eight days, the unit had no further successes until 18 March, when three victories were claimed. In a combat over Rumbeke at 1250 hrs, Hamersley attacked an Albatros D V, shooting off its bottom right hand wing. The enemy machine went down in a spin, its top wing broke away and it crashed just east of Rumbeke aerodrome, until four days previously the home of *Jasta* 7. Lts John S Griffith and C F Cunningham each claimed an Albatros out of control from the fight.

OPERATION *MICHAEL*

On Thursday 21 March the German Army launched its first offensive of the spring. At 0445 hrs over 6000 guns opened fire over a 40 mile front, the most concentrated artillery bombardment the world had yet known, and at 0800 hrs the German infantry began their advance, aided by

A group of No 60 Sqn officers in March 1918 at Bailleul. Left to right: E Thornton, holding 'Hispano', K P Campbell, J O Priestley, H D Crompton, Maj B F Moore, W J A Duncan, R K Whitney, unknown. Seated left to right: J S Griffith, C F Cunningham, H A Hamersley, J B Crompton, H A S Molyneaux

thick fog. The RFC had made extensive plans to counter the attacks, but the fog made these impossible to carry out, a situation which also frustrated the actions of the *Luftstreitkräfte*. There was a limited amount of flying on parts of Third Army front, where visibility was a little better, but it was not until midday that operations could be flown on Fifth Army front.

No 60 Sqn, serving with 11th Wing of the Second Army, was based north of the German offensive, but on 22 March the unit moved south, to the aerodrome at La Bellevue, near Doullens, to come under the orders of 13 Wing, III Bde. It was not sorry to leave Bailleul, the last two nights there it had been heavily bombed by Gothas, luckily with no damage.

On 22 March the squadron marking was again changed, to two white vertical bands painted immediately in front of the tailplane. A Flight carried the letters A to F in front of the roundel; B Flight, letters G to M on the side of the nose; C Flight carried the letters U to Z in front of the roundel.

Reinforcing the hard pressed fighter squadrons of Third and Fifth Armies, the pilots of the unit flew normal Line Patrols, and ground strafing attacks throughout the day on 24 March, the next day helping to avert a German attack at Roye, which threatened to drive a wedge between the British and French armies.

The rapid advance of the German Army had forced the evacuation of many RFC aerodromes and on 27 March the squadron moved to Fienvillers, south west of Doullens, sharing the aerodrome with Nos 11, 41,15 and 59 Sqns, with No 70 and No 1 Sqn RNAS arriving the next day. The situation at the new base was both crowded and chaotic. Communications had broken down and conflicting orders to move again, then to stay, just as the squadron's vehicles had been loaded or unloaded, added to the confusion and frustration. On a more personal note, the pilots' belongings had been lost in the retreat, as had the unit's memorabilia and trophies.

Despite these difficulties, the unit had a very successful day on 30 March. No less than nine victories were claimed during the day's fighting. Hamersley shot down an LVG which crashed into Mametz Wood at 1055 hrs and 20 minutes later fought with Albatros scouts, shooting one down out of control over Fricourt, then destroying another which crashed into the roof of a house at Hem, bursting into flames. Capts Copeland and Hegarty also claimed victories from this fight. Copeland's opponent was seen to crash into the centre of Buire village, Hegarty's at Theux. 2Lt J N Bartlett also claimed an Albatros out of control over Hem and 2Lt E R Ortner drove down another over Peronne. William Duncan and John Griffith rounded off the morning's actions by destroying an LVG over Bécourt.

By the end of March the German offensives had finally been halted. The cost to the RFC had been high. During the last ten days of the month, 85 flying personnel had been killed, 102 wounded and 52 taken POW. In addition to the human cost, and as a direct result of the low flying undertaken against the enemy troops and communications, many aircraft had returned to their aerodromes badly shot up, necessitating repair, or crash landed so badly that they were struck off strength.

Lt William 'Art' Duncan in the cockpit of Albatros DVa D5374/17 which he forced down on 1 April 1918. This Albatros was flown by Uffz Müller of *Jasta* 79 who was wounded and taken prisoner. His Albatros, given the British evaluation number G159, was at 1ASD on 20 April 1918 and flown to England the next day

THE ROYAL AIR FORCE

On 1 April 1918 the Royal Flying Corps and the Royal Naval Air Service were amalgamated to form the Royal Air Force, but the change made little difference, if any, to the hard pressed pilots and observers, and the day brought heavy casualties. The day was fine and warm, with excellent visibility, and there was a great deal of fighting in the air. The ground attack two-seaters of the *Schlachtstaffeln* were attacking British troops south of the Somme and the *Jagdstaffeln* were out in some force. In the morning A and C Flights from No 60 Sqn attacked Albatros scouts of *Jasta* 56 which were strafing British troops in the vicinity of Gentelles. One Albatros, flown by Vfw Weimer of *Jasta* 56, broke off the action and flew west, an unusual tactic. William Duncan followed and attacked Weimer who, realising his mistake, attempted to escape by turning east, but Duncan's fire had wounded him in the back and he force landed behind the British lines, near Gentelles. In an evening patrol, Capt Copeland, and Hamersley, with Lts John Priestley and F W Clark caught a DFW over Demuin at 1815 hrs, hit the observer and forced it to land. Copeland opened the scoring the next day. At 1815 hrs a mixed patrol of A and C Flight pilots saw an Albatros C type escorted by five Albatros scouts in the vicinity of Guillaucourt. After scattering the enemy scouts, Copeland attacked the two-seater, firing 200 rounds from a range of 85 ft. The German pilot put his machine into a glide and crash landed south of the village. Edgar Christie had fired at an Albatros going down in a glide, but was attacked by another, whose fire hit the SE 5a in the petrol tank, and it went down in flames between Rosieres and Vrely. Lt K Campbell's SE 5a was badly damaged and he force landed at Bertangles, possibly a claim by Vfw Johann Pütz of *Jasta* 35b. Returning to base, Frederick Clark had engine trouble and he crashed while attempting to land.

On Fifth Army front it had been noted that the *Jagdstaffeln* were now flying at high altitudes in large formations, and the fighter squadrons were given orders 'to seek out and destroy these formations'. This was a new stage in the development of air fighting tactics: two or three fighter squadrons working together in a concerted effort.

Due to bad weather, there was little flying on 4 April. The next day, low clouds, mist and rain stopped all flying. Although there were still to be some isolated outbursts of local ground fighting, it was the last day of *Kaiserschlacht*, the German spring offensive on the Somme, and preparations were set in hand for the next offensive, the battle of Lys in Flanders. No 60 Sqn, still operating over the Somme, flew ground strafing duties for the remainder of April, encountering little aerial opposition, the main air fighting now taking place in Flanders. In spite of this relative inactivity the unit lost the B Flight commander. On 11 April, B Flight took off at 1535 hrs, but extremely poor visibility forced it to return to Fienvillers. However, Capt Crawford carried on alone and while fighting a two-seater in the vicinity of Bucquoy he was attacked by Albatros scouts, shot down and killed, possibly by Vfw Otto Könnecke of *Jasta* 5 for his 16th victory. The next day the unit moved to Boffles, an aerodrome north-west of Doullens which was to be its home for the next six months. During the day, two SE 5as were hit by anti-aircraft fire, forcing both Griffith and Clark to make force landings. It was a bad omen, exacerbated by the poor accommodation the unit found at Boffles: bell tents, Nissen huts and a few dilapidated wooden huts.

Capt James Belgrave MC was posted in as B Flight commander, as replacement for Crawford, and on 23 April Capt Hamersley was sick, sent to hospital and struck off strength. He had scored 13 victories while with the unit and been awarded an MC. Capt Owen John Scholte MC was posted in as the replacement C Flight commander.

The next victories came on 6 May, William Duncan and John Griffith destroying an Albatros scout over Guillaucourt at 1915 hrs, and on the 10th Lt A W Saunders crashed a Pfalz D III over Bapaume at 1735 hrs. The weather was good on 14 May, and was to continue fine for the next ten days. Some patrols were flown but only Herbert Hegarty scored: an Albatros two-seater crashed at Moreuil at 0730 hrs. The following day more patrols were flown and four victories were claimed. Capt Scholte was the first to score, a Rumpler in flames over Lamotte at 1220 hrs for his first victory with the unit. A evening patrol by B Flight, led by Belgrave, fought with Albatros scouts over the Arras/Cambrai area. Meredith Davies sent an Albatros down in flames, Belgrave crashed another, coloured purple, and sent a second down out of control.

SE 5as of B Flight on Boffles aerodrome in April 1918 (*L Rogers*)

Capt James Dacres Belgrave. Belgrave flew first with No 45 Sqn, flying Sopwith 1½ Strutters, scoring six victories and winning an MC. He was posted to No 60 Sqn on 11 April 1918 and began scoring again on 15 May, destroying an Albatros DV. On 13 June he was missing, killed in action, after following down a two-seater. His total victories totalled to 18, the last one on the morning of his death (*C G Jefford*)

Belgrave was in action again the next morning. At 0840 hrs he forced an LVG to land north-east of Arras and Griffith and Hegarty sent its companion down to crash and burst into flames at Fampoux. In an afternoon fight with nine Albatros of *Jasta* 5 over Bapaume at 1615 hrs, Belgrave added to his success of the morning, driving one enemy scout down, smoke pouring from it. 'Pat' Saunders destroyed another, which crashed at Beaulencourt, but Vfw Fritz Rumey of the *Jasta* shot down and killed Lt H N J Proctor for his 18th victory. Two more victories for B Flight came in the early morning of 17 May. At 0500 hrs a Rumpler was found over Contalmaison and forced to land by Belgrave, Saunders, and Lewis. A Canadian from Toronto, Duncan, out alone, saw an RE 8 under attack from 15 enemy scouts over Bapaume. He immediately went to the assistance of the British two-seater, shooting off the wings of one Albatros and scattering the others, allowing the RE 8 to escape. For this action, of considerable bravery, Duncan was awarded a bar to his MC. Duncan had been Acting Flight commander of A Flight while Capt Copeland was in England, but he was now promoted to captain and given command of the Flight.

Capt Owen John Fredrick Scholte. After flying as an observer in No 18 Sqn's Vickers FB 5s, Scholte trained as a pilot and was posted to No 48 Sqn to fly Bristol Fighters. He claimed six victories with No 48 Sqn before being posted to No 60 Sqn in late April 1918, claiming another two victories and bringing his total to eight. He was killed in a motoring accident on 29 July 1918

James Belgrave, who had previously scored six victories flying two-seater Sopwith 1½ Strutters with No 45 Sqn, was now supremely confident, rapidly adding to his victories. On the morning of 18 May he was again in action, crashing both a DFW and an Albatros scout out of control over Carnoy, the first at 1115 hrs, the second 15 minutes later. On 19 May, Scholte led 12 SE 5as off the ground at 0900 hrs. Over Arras, an hour and ten minutes later, Scholte shot down a Hannover CL III in flames. There were several indecisive combats later in the patrol, and a balloon was attacked without success, but two pilots in the formation had burst propellers and were forced to return to Bellevue.

Belgrave again added to his score on 21 May driving down an LVG out of control over Courcelette at 0930 hrs, but R G Lewis had his SE so badly shot about that it was not repairable at the squadron and was returned to 2 ASD. The fine weather deteriorated in the afternoon of 23 May, with high winds, but patrols were up in the early morning. Belgrave and Saunders shared in the destruction of an Albatros over Fricourt at 0550 hrs, wounding Ltn Angermund of *Jasta* 76. Belgrave scored the unit's last victory of the month, shooting down an LVG from *Fl Abt (A)* 224 in flames. The pilot, Ltn d R Eugen Wittler, died of burns and the observer, Ltn d R Alwin Schroedter, was killed. To offset these successes, on 30 May a new pilot, Lt John Headlam, was killed during target practice, the wings of his SE 5a collapsing while diving onto the aerodrome's practice target.

No 60 Sqn had now begun to receive American pilots for training and operational experience prior to the formation of their own USAS squadrons. Many of these pilots had been used in ferrying aeroplanes to France, but at the beginning of the summer they were being posted into the fighter squadrons of the RAF in France.

It seems there was now no stopping the indefatigable Belgrave, who scored the first victory in June: a balloon 'deflated' over Pys at 0800 hrs on the first day of the month. Two days later, Duncan sent an LVG down to crash at Contalmaison at 2015 hrs, possibly a machine from *Fl Abt (A)* 211, who had an observer wounded in the day.

During the month, in addition to the usual Offensive Patrols, orders were to attack observation balloons, and over the next two days Belgrave, Saunders, Lewis, Bartlett, McCarthy, Duncan and Griffith all claimed balloons in the Mametz, Ervillers, Irles and Cherisy areas. On 5 June, Belgrave flamed a Fokker Triplane over Froyart at 1930 hrs for his 15th victory. The next day, Duncan drove down an LVG over Hamelincourt at 0540 hrs and during the remainder of the day three balloons over the areas of Pys and Susanne were attacked and forced down by Scholte, Beck, Davies and Clark. On patrol on 9 June Belgrave and Saunders attacked two Hannover C IIIs over Arras. These machines were from *Fl Abt (A)* 293 and they sent one down in flames and forced the other to land. Returning from this patrol, Gordon Duncan was injured in a crash landing, writing off his SE 5. Duncan was taken to hospital and struck off strength, but he was to rejoin the unit in July.

Four days later, James Belgrave was again in action. But his luck finally ran out. At 0445 hrs, just to the east of Albert, the SEs saw a two-seater from *Fl Abt (A)* 224. Followed by Lewis and Gordon, Belgrave dived to attack this machine, which was later reported to have crashed, but Belgrave, following it into the mist, failed to return and was later reported killed. During the action, Lewis had engine failure and landed in enemy territory between Albaincourt and Chaulnes, smashing the undercarriage of his SE 5. Henry Gordon, on his first flight over the lines, saw Lewis go down, landed nearby and ran to the crash to help, but German troops then appeared and opened fire. Gordon ran back to his machine, calling for Lewis to follow, but Lewis walked towards the enemy troops to distract them, giving Gordon a chance to take off unmolested, which he did, circling the scene to see Lewis surrounded by the enemy infantry.

With the loss of Belgrave, Capt Alfred Saunders was given temporary command of B Flight and Hegarty was given command of A Flight to allow Art Duncan, coming to the end of his tour, to fly in a freelance role. Duncan finally left the unit on 30 June.

On 19 June, ten SE 5as, led by Scholte, escorted six Sopwith Camels of No 201 Sqn in an attack on the enemy aerodrome at Boncourt, the base of *Jagdstaffeln* 21, 39 and 60. The raid was a success, but although there were no casualties a number of machines were badly damaged by ground fire.

On the last day of the month Hegarty, now promoted to captain, crashed an Albatros over Rainecourt at 0510 hrs for his seventh victory, and opened July by destroying a Halberstadt two-seater at 0840 hrs over Bray. During the patrol, John Griffith attacked a balloon, the observer taking to his parachute. Five minutes later Griffith destroyed an Albatros over Lamotte.

On 2 July, Capt Saunders led a patrol of six SEs which included two American pilots, Lts H E W Bryning and K Francis Read of the USAS. As they gained their operational height, the SEs were joined by a Sopwith Dolphin, flown by Maj Joseph Callaghan, CO of No 87 Sqn. At 1045 hrs over Bayonvillers, they saw an LVG and a Halberstadt escorted by six Pfalz D III scouts, and as the enemy formation passed over Villers-Bretonneux, Saunders led the SEs and the Dolphin down to attack it from a height advantage of 7000 ft, opening fire on the rearmost of the Pfalz, which went down out of control. Saunders then turned his attention to a Pfalz on the left of the enemy formation. Turning quickly to avoid Saunders' fire, the enemy pilot collided with his leader and both went down to crash into the Bois de Pierret. Lt Read was wounded in the fight but managed to return and land at Flesselles, the aerodrome of No 3 Sqn AFC, and was taken to hospital. After this combat, Maj Callaghan became separated from the SEs. He ran into a large number of enemy scouts from *Jasta* 13 and was shot down in flames by Ltn Büchner.

A new commander of B Flight had been posted in on 1 July: Capt Cyril Parry, who had served seven months in No 56 Sqn, had scored four victories and been awarded a DFC. Parry had flown with James McCudden in No 56 Sqn, and was an unashamed admirer of that great pilot. McCudden had advised him go home for a rest at the end of June, but Parry, feeling that he had now 'got into my stride' had decided to stay in France. Knowing in June that he was to be given command of No 60 Sqn, it is possible that McCudden arranged Parry's posting to the unit as a Flight commander. Parry was not impressed with the way things were run at his new unit. Like McCudden, a professional soldier, Parry, used to the relaxed but disciplined ways of No 56 Sqn, looked forward to McCudden's arrival: 'Mac would have sorted them out. No more lazing about in pyjamas and cigarette butts in cockpits.' Parry took out his new command for the first time at 0845 hrs on 7 July. Forty five minutes into their patrol time six Pfalz D IIIs were seen east of Bapaume at 11,000 ft, but they dived away and avoided the SEs. The next patrol had better luck. Ground signals pointed out enemy two-seaters flying at under 6000 ft in the Achiet area. Griffith crashed a DFW at Achiet-le-Grand at 1140 hrs and five minutes later American Robert K Whitney flamed another over Achiet-le-Petit, killing Sgt Joseph Brecht and Offstv Thielow of *Fl Abt* (*A*) 211. Parry took out the last patrol of the day, and during an engagement with Fokker D VIIs H A Gordon was shot down and killed over Villers Bretonneaux.

On 9 July, Maj James McCudden VC was flying out from England to take command of the squadron when he fatally crashed at Auxi-le-Chateau. The following afternoon pilots from Nos 60, 56 and other squadrons, and General Salmond, attended McCudden's funeral

Maj Cyril Marconi 'Billy' Crowe.
A 14 victory ace from No 56 Sqn,
Crowe was posted to No 60 Sqn as
commanding officer on 13 July 1918
after the death in a flying accident
of Maj James McCudden VC

at Wavans: 'poorly arranged and rushed through,' as American Paul Winslow reported. On 13 July, Maj Moore was promoted to Lt Col and posted to command of 1 ASD. The unit's new CO was Maj Cyril Marconi 'Billy' Crowe MC.

Hegarty, the A Flight commander, was posted to HE on 16 July. His replacement as flight commander was Capt George Dell-Clarke, but it was a short lived appointment. Taking off in Hegarty's SE, Dell-Clarke crashed while stunting over the aerodrome and was killed. Capt John Edgcombe Doyle was posted in from No 56 Sqn to take over the Flight. Engine trouble caused another loss on 17 July. Lt George L du Cros crashed on take-off, suffered cuts to his face, was taken to hospital and struck off strength.

In patrols on 16 July, two balloons were destroyed by 'Little' Whitney and Bryning and on 18 July, at 0500 hrs, Whitney attacked a DFW of *Fl Abt* (*A*) 208 flying at 1000 ft south of Boiry Notre Dame. Three bursts caused the two-seater to break up in mid-air. Ltn d R Wilhelm Bringmann and Vfw Paul Liebau were both killed. Returning to the

Lt G L du Cros was injured in this crash of SE 5a E1306 due to engine failure on 7 July 1918 (*L Rogers*)

lines at 600 ft, the American's SE was hit by ground fire, but he managed to return and land safely. John Sharpe Griffith was not so lucky. Also hit by ground fire, he crashed in a cornfield near Fortel. Slightly injured, he was sent to hospital and struck off strength. Griffith, an American from Seattle, had joined the RFC in 1917 and had served with No 60 Sqn since February 1918, scoring seven victories and winning a DFC.

In an early patrol on 22 July, a number of enemy fighters from *Jasta 32* were attacked at 0540 hrs over Aveluy Wood. Capt Doyle sent a Pfalz D III down out of control and Lt John R Anderson forced another to land, but in the fighting John E C MacVicker was shot down and killed by Ltn Emil Koch for his fifth victory. Thirty five minutes later a patrol led by Lt Frederick W Clark shared in the destruction of a balloon south of Grevillers for the unit's last victory of the month. Landing back at base, two SE 5as were written off in bad landings. Lt F W McCarthy's machine was badly damaged and Clark overshot and ran into a gun pit, overturning his SE.

On 24 July the American Lt H E Bryning was transferred to No 57 Sqn and was replaced by another USAS pilot, Lt Charles France. Four days later their fellow American, Lt Lawrence Loughran, was practising air to ground gunnery when his SE spun in and he was killed.

Another casualty was caused by engine trouble on 29 July. Five days previously Cyril Parry had taken charge of a new Viper-engined SE 5a D360. He was unhappy with the engine of this machine and had been working on it during the afternoon. Taking off on a test, the engine cut out soon after take-off. The SE hit the ground, cartwheeled several times, and was completely demolished. Parry was seriously injured, spending the remainder of the war in hospital.

While Parry had been working on his engine, Maj Crowe had invited him to attend a dinner party that night at Dieppe, being hosted by Maj Bowman, CO of No 41 Sqn. Crowe and Scholte were leaving that afternoon in the squadron's Crossley, and Parry, wanting to work on his engine, declined. After the party, Crowe decided to drive back himself, his driver being unwell. Along with Crowe and Capt Scholte,

Maj Cyril Foggin and Capts Soden, McCall and Moline went along for a lift back to their respective squadrons. It was 1145 hrs, the night was moonlit but misty, and Crowe, mistaking a gap in the trees lining the road as being straight on, missed the turn and the car ran off the road. While recovering in hospital, Frank Soden, now a Flight commander in No 41 Sqn, wrote: 'The driver mistook a gap in the trees for a road, with the result that we hit about three trees and smashed the car to blazes. I remember a skid, a crash and tons of stars and then I came to in a cornfield about 20 yards from the crash. I couldn't speak for about ten minutes as all my wind was knocked out. We went back further up the road and found three fellows on the road, two very badly smashed. The other fellow who is in the bed next to me now, smashed his *wooden* leg and cut his face. I was sitting with Major Foggin on my knee and another fellow, Capt Sholte, on my right. These were the two badly smashed up ones, both fractured skulls, and I'm very sorry to say that they died in hospital this morning. There are three of us left in hospital, all as sore as we can be, and with a few bits of skin taken off in places. Rotten end for poor old "Froggy".' Crowe was court-martialled for driving a car without orders, given a severe reprimand and was reduced in rank to captain. Maj Alexander Clarke was posted in as Commanding officer, arriving on 14 August.

THE BATTLE OF AMIENS – THE BEGINNING OF THE END

The part to be played by the RAF in preparations for the coming offensive, scheduled to begin on 8 August, included intensive bombing and ground attacks. One element of this programme was low level bombing attacks on German aerodromes and, on 1 August, one such raid was made on the aerodrome at Epinoy, the home of two Bavarian *Jagdstaffeln*, Nos 23b and 35b. The Sopwith Camels of No 3 Sqn and the SE 5as of No 56 Sqn were to carry out low level bombing, with top cover, in ascending steps of 1000 ft, by the SE 5as of No 60 Sqn and the Sopwith Dolphins of No 87 Sqn. Higher still were the Bristol Fighters of No 11 Sqn, who were to photograph the results of the raid and protect any stragglers from enemy fighters. The attack was highly successful. Sixteen enemy aircraft were reported to have been destroyed on the ground, with sheds and hangars set on fire, the smoke rising to 10,000 ft. Sixty five British aircraft took part in the raid and all returned safely. There were no engine failures, and Brig Gen Longcroft, who had flown a Camel above the attack, considered the success of the operation had been due to a great extent to 'the excellent work of the WOs, NCOs and men'. The pilots of the top cover had also joined in the low level attacks. Alexander Beck commented: 'Machines set on fire, 250 rounds at GTs and transport. Aerodrome bombed to hell – everybody back.'

In the evening, an Offensive Patrol led by Capt A W Saunders, who was Parry's replacement as B Flight commander, was in combat with Fokker D VIIs over Bapaume, Saunders claiming one out of control at 2020 hrs. On 3 August, Saunders flamed a balloon over Martinpuich at 1700 hrs and Beck and the Flight claimed another an hour and 20 minutes later over Sapignies. The next day, Witney and Beck destroyed another balloon at 0625 hrs over Suzanne-Le-Sars, the observer

Capt Alexander Beck. Beck joined No 60 Sqn at the end of July 1917, but after three weeks, during which he flew 13 patrols, his parents discovered that he was in France, informed the authorities that he was under age and he was posted back to England. In March 1918, having reached the required age, Beck rejoined the unit, became a Flight commander, won a DFC, and served until the end of the war, scoring 11 victories

taking to his parachute, and at 0715 hrs the pair drove down a DFW over the Albert/Combles area. On 6 and 7 August, pilots carried out low level attacks throughout the day, in one instance to drown out the noise of over 300 tanks moving forward for the imminent battle.

At 0420 hrs on the morning of 8 August, the battle of Amiens opened with an overwhelming artillery barrage, 2000 guns opening fire on a 20 mile front, from Morlancourt to La Neuville. The ground forces quickly followed the lifting of the barrage, advancing through heavy mist and meeting little opposition. The early mist hampered work by the RAF until 0900 hrs, when it cleared and air operations could begin. Patrols from No 60 Sqn were in action by noon, Saunders and Beck attacking a Fokker D VII over Roulers at 15,000 ft. Saunders overshot in his attack, but Beck made no mistake, shooting it down in a spin to crash by the side of the Amiens to Roye road. Beck then had engine trouble and force landed at Senlis, but Saunders carried on and attacked a two-seater with a white tail, which went down through the clouds out of control, possibly a machine from *Fl Abt* (*A*) 241, which reported a crew killed over Rosières during the day. Capt Gordon Duncan (a Scot, and no relation to the Canadian William Duncan) claimed his first victory with the unit with a Fokker D VII crashed over Peronne at 1400 hrs, and during an evening patrol John Doyle and Robert Whitney crashed a Hannover CL at Foucaucourt at 1640 hrs, reporting that the German crew bailed out. Ten minutes later Whitney and Clark flamed a DFW over Estrees and Doyle crashed another Hannover CL in the same area at 1655 hrs. Offsetting these victories, 2Lt James G 'Shorty' Hall USAS had been shot down and killed, possibly by a crew from *Schlachtstaffeln* 11 or 27b, both of which claimed SE 5as in the area.

8 August was the final turning point of the war, a day referred to by Ludendorff as 'the black day in the German Army … it put the decline of our fighting power beyond all doubt. The war must be ended.'

The unit had a very successful day on 9 August. In the morning patrols, at 0820 hrs, Capts Doyle, Whitney, Clark and A N Westergaard all drove down balloons over Etaing and 15 minutes later Doyle and Whitney destroyed a Hannover CL over Croisilles. The fighting in the afternoon brought five more victories. In a fight over the Nesles/Chaulnes area at 1520 hrs, Harold Buckley and Gordon Duncan each crashed a Fokker D VII over Marchelpot and Nesles respectively, and ten minutes later Duncan sent another down out of control over Chaulnes. At 1545 hrs, Saunders crashed two more Fokker D VIIs, one over Chaulnes and another a few minutes later over Nesles. On 10 August, Duncan crashed another Fokker D VII over Foucaucourt at 0645 hrs, but Harold Buckley was wounded in the knee during the fighting. He landed safely back at base, was taken to hospital at Rouen and invalided to HE. The next day Doyle and Duncan shared in the destruction of a pair of two-seaters over Chaulnes at 0950 hrs, but enemy scouts from *Jasta* 37 intervened and Ltn Meyer of the *Jasta* wounded Canadian Robert Whitney in the wrist. He managed to land at No 48 Sqn's aerodrome at Bertangles and was taken to hospital. In his last month with the unit, Whitney had claimed five victories plus four balloons. He was later awarded a DFC.

Lt G F C Caswell had rounded off the day's victories on 11 August with an LVG crashed at Ervillers at 1640 hrs, and the next day saw the first victory for another of the unit's American pilots, when Oliver 'Spike' Johnson USAS shared a victory with the Canadian Westergaard, forcing a two-seater to land at Croisilles just after noon. An evening patrol on 13 August attacked five Fokker D VIIs north of Chaulnes, but an additional 12 dived into the fight. Lt John Anderson was shot down in flames and killed by Vfw Otto Fruhner of *Jasta* 26 for his 15th victory, and a new pilot, Canadian E J C McCracken was shot down and taken POW by Hptm Bruno Loerzer, commanding officer of *Jagdgeschwader* III, for his 29th victory.

On 14 August a morning patrol led by Doyle was in action with Albatros scouts over Guemappe and claimed three victories. At 0945 hrs Doyle and Beck each crashed an Albatros at Guemappe, and Beck was credited with a Hannover CL destroyed over Riencount, although his logbook makes no mention of this last, merely stating: 'OP. Attacked Albatros scouts at Guemappe. One crashed by Doyle and one by me.'

Capt Alfred 'Pat' Saunders, the B Flight commander, left for HE on 15 August. A veteran of the Dardanelles campaign, while in the Royal Field Artillery, he had served four months with No 60 Sqn, had scored 12 victories and been awarded a DFC. B Flight was taken over by 19-year-old Frederick Clark, for some strange reason nicknamed 'Suzie'.

The squadron was now fully up to strength, with 25 pilots, although a third of these were still in training. Nineteen SE 5as were on charge, 14 Viper-engined, the remainder powered by Hispano-Suiza engines.

BATTLE FOR BAPAUME

Over-riding the wishes of Marshal Foch, who wanted the next Allied offensive to be against the German positions at Roye/Chaulnes, Haig decided that it should be by the British First and Third Armies in an offensive at Bapaume, to begin on 27 August. No 60 Sqn was to be part of the RAF air support during the battle and the preparations began on 17 August. Preliminary fighting before the main battle was a localised attack on 21 August to capture the Arras to Albert railway line, and as one of the three fighter squadrons of III Brigade, No 60 Sqn was to support VI Corps by low level attacks on ground targets. Beginning at 30 minutes after zero hour the unit was ordered to take off in pairs, in half hourly intervals. A light rain fell on the night before the attack, continuing after dawn, and a morning mist failed to clear until 1100 hrs. When operations began, the unit seemed to have ignored the orders to fly in pairs and flew in sections of four throughout the day. The first casualty from the ground strafing was Lt Stephen Keen. He was last seen over Ervillers at 1330 hrs, flying at 500 ft. He was hit by ground fire, crashed, and was pulled unconscious from his SE 5a by British troops. He was taken to a casualty station, but his skull was fractured and he died seven days later without having regained consciousness. Capt Frederick Clark, with Lts Bartlett, Charles France, and F E Smith took off at 1405 hrs. They fared little better. Bombing gun pits and horse transport of the Ervillers to Sapignies road, Clark's SE 5 was so badly damaged that he was forced to land only 200 yards west of the front line, overturning his SE, and Smith returned to Boffles with a badly damaged machine. Of the four pilots who took off at 1710 hrs, only one failed to return to base. After attacking targets in the Behagnies-Sapignies-Mory area, Westergaard became separated from Beck, Johnson and Sinclair, and attacked a two-seater. During the fight his compensator refused to open fully, he lost power and the enemy observer scored hits on the SE, forcing Westergaard to land at Bellevue. The low level operations continued the next day, but after dropping their bombs on targets near Croisilles, Doyle, Beck and Oliver attacked a balloon, driving it down, the observer taking to his parachute. From midday normal OPs were flown and at 1730 hrs Doyle, Beck and Oliver destroyed a balloon over Haucourt, with Beck and France destroying another a little later over Cagnicourt. In late evening low level attacks, F W McCarthy's machine was hit in the petrol tank by anti-aircraft fire and he force landed in a field near Gouy-en-Artois at 2000 hrs. Two more victories were scored the next day, the opening day of the battle of Bapaume. Doyle crashed a dark-painted DFW at 0955 hrs at Croisilles and M D 'Sink' Sinclair sent its orange-coloured companion down out of control. Later in the day Clark's SE was hit by ground fire and he force landed at Bavincourt.

Alexander Beck in the cockpit of an SE 5a, with 2Lt H J O Barnett. Barnett, known as 'The Fat Old Bean', was first with the unit in November 1917, but was injured in the eye by a broken glass during a Mess party. He returned to the unit in June 1918 as Gunnery Officer and served until the end of hostilities (*L Rogers*)

Alexander Beck's SE 5a D6945 U of C Flight at Boffles. Beck scored his first four victories with the unit in this aeroplane (L Rogers)

On 24 August two more balloons were driven down by McCarthy and S C Millar, and Beck and Blessley drove down a Hannover CL, wounding or killing the observer. Two SEs failed to return: Lt France's machine was hit by ground fire and he force landed at Achiet-le-Grand. McCarthy's SE was also damaged by ground fire, and he landed at La Bellvue, the base of No 32 Sqn.

No further victories were claimed until the last day of the month. Despite the weather – low clouds and rain – a ten strong patrol was out and Beck and R A Oliver caught an LVG near Inchy. Oliver recorded: 'Ten of us caught a poor old two-seater just our side of the lines. I was flying on Beck's right and we went down together and came up under his tail. The other Flight had gone ahead to cut him off from getting back. We both started to shoot about the same time and pieces started to fly off his tailplane and elevator. He took a nose-dive and kept on going. Beck very kindly gave me credit for an assist on that one and we each got a half.' Balloons were attacked in the middle of the day, two being driven down by Doyle, Oliver Johnson and Gordon Duncan, the observers bailing out. A patrol leaving at 1810 hrs fought with Fokker D VIIs over Bapaume. Lt J E Smith's SE was badly damaged in the fighting and he was forced to return, landing at 1930 hrs.

The unit's casualty rate during the month had been low, with two pilots killed, two wounded and one taken prisoner, but it was not typical of the RAF as a whole. The fighter squadrons had made tremendous efforts during the offensives in August, playing a not inconsiderable part in their success, but the cost had been high. From the opening of the battle of Amiens on 8 August to the end of the month, 72 pilots had been killed in action, 53 wounded, and 62 – many of whom were also wounded – taken prisoner. The cost in equipment was also high. Nearly 80 aircraft had been shot up, badly damaged and forced to land while carrying out low level attacks, the price of closely supporting the ground forces. The *Luftstreitkräfte* had fewer losses, but unlike the RAF could not absorb them. The shortage of raw material placed it in a critical position until the end of the war.

THE LAST BATTLES

The next British offensive was to be attacks by First and Third Army against the Drocourt Quéant switch line. Orders were that the fighter squadrons were to carry out ground strafing operations throughout the day, leaving their aerodromes in squadron strength at first light. These attacks were fully organised. Pilots no longer had *carte blanche* to attack any targets they chose, these were now carefully selected to give maximum support to the ground troops.

The weather on the first day of September was fine, but with a strong wind. In the morning, Capts Doyle and Duncan, along with Lt Johnson shot down two balloons over Ruyaulcourt at 1010 hrs. The next morning, Lts Sinclair and McCarthy caught two LVGs in the Ecourt St Quentin area at 1000 hrs and McCarthy damaged one over the village at 1005 hrs. Sinclair chased his a little further to the north-east, finally crashing it over Brunemont ten minutes later. In an afternoon patrol Johnson shot down an Albatros scout which crashed at Marquion at 1910 hrs.

On 3 September, flying an escort for the low flying Camels of No 3 Sqn, five Fokker D VIIs were attacked over Inchy, Doyle sending one down to crash by the village at 1010 hrs. During the fighting, Lt J F M Kerr's SE was hit in the engine and he was forced to land. An early morning patrol on 4 September was in combat at 0630 hrs with Fokker D VIIs of *Jasta* 36. Eleven SE 5as of the unit were flying top cover for the Camels of 148th Aero Squadron USAS and attacked five Fokkers of the *Jasta* which were about to attack the Camels. The Fokkers were then joined by an additional five, but the arrival of SE 5as of No 64 Sqn evened up the odds. A Fokker on the tail of McEntegart was shot down by Sinclair and it crashed at Raillincourt. Oliver Johnson shot down another, which spun down in flames to crash at Epinoy. Johnson then came under attack by five Fokkers, which drove him down to ground level, where his engine cut out and his propeller was shot off. Ten enemy aircraft were between Johnson and the front lines, but he dived steeply, under the Fokkers, and force landed near Queant. Ltn Quandt of *Jasta* 36 was awarded Johnson as his 15th victory. Gordon Duncan also destroyed one of the Fokkers, which crashed at Cambrai, for his 6th victory. *Jasta* 36 reported two pilots killed over Abancourt, just under four miles to the north-east of the claims, probably where the fighting began.

The next morning Maj Clarke called John Doyle into the squadron office, to tell him that No 57 Sqn were to bomb targets east of Cambrai that afternoon: 'It's about thirty five miles over and they want an escort. Take ten machines. You might as well fly over to lunch with them, then you can fix up the details.' Doyle was due to leave for England the next day and this seemed a pleasant and uneventful way of passing his last day in France, so he flew to No 57 Sqn's aerodrome for lunch and discussed the proposed raid. Five DH 4 bombers were to carry out the raid and Doyle agreed to rendezvous with them at 13,000 ft over Doullens.

This SE 5a, believed to be E3919, was crash landed by Lt M D Sinclair after combat damage on 5 September 1918 (*L Rogers*)

At half past two, Doyle and his Flight met the DH 4s and the whole formation headed east. The heavily loaded bombers climbed slower than the fighters but, at the altitude at which the formation was flying as it approached its objective, Doyle knew that once the DH 4s had released their bombs they would be faster than the SE5s on their flight home:

'So I wanted a bit of height up my sleeve, so to speak. When they laid their eggs I was about four thousand feet above them. They headed west, but I flew on a little way so that when I did turn I could see them over the leading edge of my lower plane, which meant that I was some way behind them. It was a good strategic position as it turned out, because the pilots of four Fokker biplanes, which I presently noticed climbing up under the "Fours" were quite unaware of the presence of my escort.

'Most British pilots have had experience of the various traps the Germans used to set so skilfully in order to lure unsuspecting airmen to their doom. This was the first occasion, however, as far as I was concerned, when the position was reversed. I was ideally placed. But I decided I must not be in too great a hurry. I must wait till they were nibbling at the bait with their attention thus fully occupied. So I closed my radiator shutter and rocked my machine slowly to attract the attention of my patrol. I wound my tail wheel forward and held the bus up with the stick while I watched the Fokkers' progress with interest. The way they could overhaul the "Fours" was an education.

'Then I saw some tracer leave the leading Fokker. It was long range shooting but I knew I could not further delay matters. And at that moment a red Very light curved into the sky from one of the "Fours". This was clearly my summons, but I hoped it would not cause the Huns to look round. I let my stick forward and my bus dropped from under me. I looked back. With one exception my patrol appeared to be unaware that I was diving for they remained above. The exception, Lt Rayner, was close on my right. Soon we were down behind the Fokkers and rushing at them. We had the two rear machines respectively of that formation of five in our sights. It was essential in this, our first dive, that we should make certain of our men before the cat was out of the bag, and so we held our fire until the last possible minute, then opened up simultaneously. I can clearly recall being aware that tracer left Rayner's guns at the same instant that I pressed my own triggers. I was also aware of a sheet of flame in the right-hand Fokker's cockpit. My own target shot up vertically and stalled.

'We were now below the level of the "Fours" for the Fokkers were still climbing up to them. My intention had been to get in my first burst and then zoom up to take stock of the situation. But I had been very close to my man when he reared up and I had to shoot my stick forward to pass below him. I was still travelling very fast and that put me in a dive again. I got the leader in my sight and let go another burst. This time the Fokker did a flick left turn and dived in a southerly direction. I did some rapid – and it seems faulty – thinking.

'There were fifteen of us Britishers in the sky. We had accounted for two of the Jerries for certain. I thought I had another but wanted to make sure. Already I had turned south and was diving after my man. I had forgotten about my leave for the moment. There were two more Fokkers about, but, thought I, they will be well marked. I got in another burst and held it while I tried to close up, but the only result was that my man went into a still steeper dive, always flying straight. So I knew I had got him. But the laugh was on me also, for a burst

Personnel of A Flight in the summer of 1918. Standing left to right: Sgt Scammel, Corps: Barrett, Carmen, Wormald. Warrant officers: Edwards, Robinson, Morris. Corps: Hutcheson, Nash, Haworth, Duncan, Bird. Sitting left to right: Sgt Haslins, Lts B S Johnston, H S Stuart-Smith, J W Rayner, J E Doyle, S A Thomson. Of the five pilots in this photograph, S A Thomson was killed in action on 5 September, John Doyle was made POW on 5 September, and Stuart-Smith was killed in action on 15 September (*L Rogers*)

of close range stuff crashed into my SE at that moment. I think one's brain works at extra speed on such occasions. On looking back, at any rate, that is the impression I get. A result is a slowing up of the action, and so I will give my recollections in slow motion.

'A bullet cracked past just clear of the cockpit; a second went through the instrument board into the tank; the third struck my head just behind the ear and cut the buckle of my chin strap, which fell slowly down. Two more cracks and then a terrific concussion. I was pressed against the side of the cockpit, unable to move, while the 'plane fell headlong, turning on its axis as it did so. Still I was pinned against the side. Petrol was pouring on to me and I managed to depress the switch. Obviously something had broken; but what? I looked along each wing but could see nothing wrong. The twisting, patterned landscape ahead was growing in size ominously. I looked round at my tail, which seemed intact. But full left rudder was on! I must have been falling at over two hundred miles an hour, so the strain on tail and fuselage can be imagined. I looked into the cockpit for the first time and realised the trouble.

'Naturally, as the aeroplane was standing on its nose all my weight was on the rudder bar. But it was my left leg which was carrying most of the weight, my right flying boot being folded back, but with the foot still in the stirrup. The cause of the machine's strange behaviour was instantly clear. That concussion I had experienced had been due to a bullet smashing my shinbone and at the same time paralysing the nerve. I grabbed the boot and dragged it out of the stirrup then pulled with my left leg and the aeroplane responded immediately. I looked up past my tail and got a head-on impression of two Fokkers diving after me. Instinct warned me that there was an ominous meaning in the speed with which they were following me down. They were not, I surmised, solicitous for my welfare! The ground was near but I dived again to maintain my lead and flattening out hurriedly made a landing of sorts in what appeared to be a park.

'When the SE had stopped bouncing and come to a rest, I threw off my belt and stood on the seat. A burst of fire from the leading Fokker spattered around me, but I was not hit. When this had stopped I jumped to the ground, tried to take a step and of course fell. There was another long burst of firing from above and I lay without moving. Bullets seemed to be smacking into the grass in a circle round my body but again I was not touched. Two German Tommies had approached me as near as seemed advisable, and when the firing ceased I got up and hopped over to them. I thought it would be healthier there, and it was. I showed them the condition of my leg by flapping it at them and they helped me away and presently laid me on the ground, where I was soon surrounded by a little crowd of sympathetic French women and children. Then a German in flying kit joined the group and I knew he must be one of the Fokker pilots. There was a fierce altercation between him and the crowd. The German was trying to drown all other voices by the power of his own. I discovered he had been questioned as to why he had fired at a prisoner, and his reply was that I had killed his friend. I learnt later that three Fokkers had been brought down, but that was only partial compensation for that leave. The head wound was

Capt John Edgcombe Doyle. Born in Somerset, Doyle served with his regiment in France for a year before transferring to the RFC in September 1916. He was posted to No 56 Sqn on 27 March 1918 and served with that unit until 16 July when he was posted to No 60 Sqn as the A Flight commander. Doyle scored nine victories with the unit and was awarded a DFC. He was shot down and made POW on 5 September 1918. In this post-war photograph he proudly wears his RFC tie

superficial – so at least I always stoutly maintain – but for three days gangrene crept up my leg, and then it was amputated high up. It was touch and go for me by that time. But I had several narrow squeaks on that trip, of which two bullets in the petrol tank were not the least. Still, all's well that ends well.'

The Fokker D VIIs in this action were from *Jasta* 4. Doyle was the victim of Ltn Egon Koepsch for his eighth victory. One of the Fokkers shot down was Ltn Joachin von Winterfeld – the friend mentioned by Koepsch. Winterfeld had bailed out from his flaming aeroplane, but his parachute caught fire. Uffz Josef Döerflinger successfully bailed out of his damaged Fokker. Six Fokkers were awarded from this combat: Doyle with one in flames and one out of control. J W Rayner was also credited with one in flames – observed by Doyle – and on another out of control, as was Gordon Duncan. During the fighting, American Robert Blessley USAS was wounded in the leg but managed to return to Boffles. Blessley was the second casualty of the day. Canadian Samuel A Thomson had been shot down and killed in the morning by Offstv Josef Mai of *Jasta* 5 for his 25th victory. John 'Bill' Rayner was given command of A Flight.

Bad weather, ground strafing and attacks on balloons over the next ten days saw no further victories until 15 September. An evening patrol led

Lt Robert C W Blessley USAS. One of eight pilots of the United States Air Service to be posted to the unit in the summer of 1918 for operational experience, Blessley was wounded in action on 5 September 1918 (L Rogers)

by Harry Stuart-Smith, and including Johnson and Gordon Duncan, were in combat with eight Fokker D VIIs over Fontaine-Notre-Dame. Stuart-Smith's SE was seen to go down, with one wing broken off, to crash near Bourlon Wood. This patrol was Gordon Duncan's last with the unit. He was posted as a Flight commander to No 56 Sqn two days later.

The ground offensives were now going extremely well, the troops advancing rapidly, and in their support orders were to bomb and strafe enemy positions on the 6th Corps front. To facilitate this support, No 201 Sqn flew their Camels into Baizieux aerodrome on 17 September, with No 60 Sqn flying in on returning from its first patrols from Boffles. No 148th Aero USAS flew their Camels in on 18 September. No 60 Sqn was to provide top cover for the Camels, which were to fly low level strafing attacks. On 17 September, during a midday patrol from the new base A Flight were in action with Fokker D VIIs over Marquoin and Lt Joe E Smith was shot down and killed. On 18 September the unit lost its longest serving pilot when the B Flight commander Capt Frederick

Clark was posted to HE. His replacement as Flight commander was Capt Alexander Beck. Oliver Johnson USAS was also posted out, going to Issoudun to pass on his experience to his fellow Americans still in training there. There was little flying on 19 September, a day of low clouds, wind and rain. Conditions were much the same the next day, but in the bright intervals the *Jagdstaffeln* were out in some force and there was a great deal of air fighting. An early morning patrol had left Baizieux before dawn, using the flames from their exhausts to keep together. A new pilot, Lt Fred Battle, was very short and was sitting on three cushions to improve his view. This was to prove fortunate. Over the Havrincourt to Marcoing road the patrol was attacked by a large force of Fokker D VIIs from *Jasta* 27. Capt Bernard 'Bins' McEntegart, leading the formation, had seen the Camels of No 201 Sqn flying below them and he dived to bring the SEs and their attackers down to their height. Unfortunately, the Fokkers were too fast and opened fire before the SEs could reach the Camels. George F C Caswell was wounded, forced to land and was taken prisoner. Battle was hit in the thigh and buttocks, but the extra cushion impeded the bullet and saved him from serious injury. He flew into the cloud cover, went down to ground level and landed at Frémicourt aerodrome.

THE BATTLE OF THE CANAL DU NORD

Orders issued by HQ 13th Wing for the support of Third Army in the coming battle detailed that No 60 Sqn were to fly top cover for the ground strafing Camels of Nos 201, 3, and No 148 Aero Sqn of the USAS. On 27 September the British armies attacked towards Cambrai and St Quentin. During the air fighting above the battle, enemy fighters were driven down to the Camels by the SE 5as of the unit and the American pilots were able to claim some successes. On 28 September Alexander Beck destroyed an LVG over Cambrai at 0825 hrs, the last victory of the month for the squadron, confirmed by pilots of No 59 Sqn.

During the month the *Jagdstaffeln* had been both active and successful. Many of the German pilots were now veteran combat pilots, flying the superb BMW-powered Fokker D VII and the new Pfalz D XII. These factors made them formidable opponents for the Allied fighter pilots, many of whom were novice pilots in the rapidly expanding RAF and this is reflected in the casualty figures for the month, the largest suffered since the bloody April of 1917. The penultimate month of the war would see no let up in the fiercely contested air fighting, some days seeing the heaviest and most intense air fighting of the war.

PRELUDE TO VICTORY

Since the middle of July 1918 to the end of September, the German armies lost heavily in men killed and wounded, plus 250,000 men taken prisoner, almost 4000 guns and 250,000 machine guns. Ludendorff informed the *Reichstag* that the war was lost and that a peace offer must be made 'at once: every twenty four hours can only make the situation worse'. The bitter struggle of four long years was finally coming to an end.

To the men still involved in the day-to-day fighting, the end of the war seemed as remote as ever. Although the Allied offensives of August and September had been largely successful, the ground forces were still meeting stiff resistance during the last days of September. It seemed that the spirit and fighting capacity of the German troops was unimpaired. But this impression was false: the German troops *were* demoralised, both by their recent defeats on the ground and by constant attacks from the air, and in October the German armies suddenly began to show the first signs of its eventual disintegration.

However, the fighting in the air was still intense. The first day of the month was fine. Enemy activity was described as 'moderate' but RAF squadrons were active throughout the day, bombing the all-important rail links which supplied the German Army.

On 3 October a morning patrol from No 60 Sqn was in combat with Fokker D VIIs over the Esnes area at 0815 hrs and Capt Beck and Canadian L Havill Smith were each awarded a Fokker out of control over the village. In the afternoon, the unit flew an escort for the DH 4s of No 57 Sqn, bombing the railway stations of Bertry and Le Cateau. It had been observed that the *Jagdstaffeln* were now flying in large formations, gaining a height advantage before making any attempt to attack bombers, and it had been decided that the most effective way of protecting these was not close up, but operating in the vicinity, within sight of them. Following such tactics, formations of opposing fighters would often fly parallel to each other, not attacking until one had gained the advantage of height. During the afternoon escort of No 57 Sqn, Beck's formation was being out-climbed by Fokker D VIIs, but S J Mason turned across and attacked one, shooting it down in flames over Malincourt at 1445 hrs.

Weather conditions were now changeable, but ground-strafing sorties were flown when possible. On 8 October, Beck had dropped his bombs but climbing away his SE was hit in the petrol tank and fuel poured out

The officers' Mess at Baizieux, October 1918 (L Rogers)

SE 5as of A Flight on Baizieux aerodrome in October 1918. SE 5a D6953, marked A, was flown by Capt J W Rayner who scored all five of his victories with the unit in this machine (*L Rogers*)

over the hot exhaust. Fortunately there was no fire and Beck landed at Léchelles, No 15 Sqn's aerodrome. Fifty minutes later Stanley Mason also force landed after his machine was hit by ground fire The next day Beck flamed an LVG over Bohain at 1140 hrs, possibly a machine from *Fl Abt* (*A*) 245. For the next few days the weather stopped nearly all flying and Beck took the opportunity to fly to the wreckage of the LVG and souvenir both the signal and the Parabellum guns from the gunner's cockpit.

On 14 October the unit moved to the advanced landing ground at Beugnâtre, landing there after the first patrols of the day, the Camels of No 148 Aero Squadron USAS following them in. No 201 Sqn also flew in their Camels, No 59 Sqn moving out to make room. At this time the last of the Hispano-engined SE 5as were replaced, leaving the unit fully equipped with Viper-engined machines. The weather deteriorated still further over the unit's area of operations and there were no combats until the 22nd, Beck again being the only successful pilot, with a Halberstadt forced to land in No-Man's-Land at 1615 hrs. Beck later salvaged the cross from this machine and had it framed. The following day the weather was better and there was a great deal of fighting. A and B Flights were both out in the afternoon and were in action with a mixed enemy formation of Fokker D VIIs and Siemens-Schuckert D IVs. Capts Rayner and McCarthy each claimed a Fokker D VII out of control over Selesches at 1430 hrs, with Beck destroying an LVG in the same area 40 minutes later.

The morning of 25 October brought five more victories in the morning patrols over the Berlaimont area. At 0950 hrs Rayner and his Flight attacked five Fokker D VIIs of *Jasta* 5. Rayner flamed one and sent another down out of control; Stanley Mason and Evan Burbidge claimed one each as out of control. The Fokker attacked by Lt Havill Smith went down smoking and the pilot bailed out of his machine, which finally crashed. Smith's Vickers gun was out of action with a faulty Constantinesco gear; he had used an entire drum of his Lewis gun firing into the Fokker and he now had considerable difficulty placing a fresh drum. Defenceless, he was attacked by seven enemy fighters and took violent evasive action, going down to ground level.

Two of the enemy pilots stayed with him, began to hit the SE with accurate bursts of fire, and Smith force landed near what he mistakenly took to be French troops. He was behind the lines and was taken prisoner, claimed by Vfw Treiber for his seventh and last victory. Rayner and Smith's victory was possibly a duplicate claim for Uffz Praclic, who bailed out of his blazing machine. Vfw Böhm was forced to break away during the fighting, due to his seat collapsing, and was probably one of the out of control claims made.

The only positive victory on 26 October was an LVG crashed at Le Quesnoy. At 1325 hrs Beck and Lt Claude Orpen both attacked this two-seater, which broke up in mid-air. The observer bailed out of his disintegrating machine but his parachute failed to open. This LVG was possibly from *Fl Abt* (*A*) 207, which reported Ltn Helmann and Ltn Schiplit both killed during the day. Alex Beck, having now flown for seven months with the unit was at the end of his tour, but given the choice of a posting to HE or staying with the squadron he

Capt John William Rayner. Rayner was commissioned in the Northumberland Fusiliers in September 1915. He later transferred to the RFC and served as an observer in No 52 Sqn. After pilot training he was posted to No 60 Sqn on 25 August 1918. He was given command of A Flight after the loss of Capt Doyle on 5 September (*L Rogers*)

elected to stay, no doubt sensing that the end of the war was in sight. He relinquished the command of B Flight and took up a roving commission. On 28 October on one of his solo flights, Beck drove an LVG down over Valenciennes at 1250 hrs. A morning patrol, flown to meet and escort home the DH 4s of No 57 Sqn, lost Lionel Stockwell. Stockwell, the rearmost SE in the formation, was hit by Fokker D VIIs which dived on the formation from out of the sun. He force landed behind the lines and was taken prisoner. Another escort flown for No 57 Sqn the next day attacked two formations of Fokker D VIIs at 1440 hrs. Mason crashed one over Landrecies, and Beck and Burbidge each claimed a Fokker out of control over Mormal. On 30 October, Capt B McEntegart scored the last victory of the month. With SE 5as from another squadron he destroyed an LVG over Mormal at 0930 hrs.

Orders had been received to change aerodromes yet again, this time to Bévillers, six miles east of Cambrai, but these were changed to Quiévy, three miles further east of the town, and the move was made on the last day of the month. The first patrol from the new base took off at 0800 hrs on 1 November. Six Fokkers were seen, but were too far away to attack. Later in the day a patrol led by Beck attacked 13 Fokker D VIIs north-west of Bavai. McCarthy sent one down out of control over the town at 1535 hrs and 25 minutes later he joined Beck and Newth in destroying another over Mormal Wood. Despite the poor weather, Beck was out alone the next day and scored the unit's last victory of the war. He attacked a pair of LVGs north-east of Le Quesnoy at 0830 hrs, hitting one in the petrol tank and forcing it to land. It was Beck's 15th victory and he went on leave the following day.

On 9 November, pilots flew over 51 hours and fired nearly 400 rounds at the retreating German troops. During one patrol, by McCarthy,

Capts Rayner (left) and B McEntegart, autumn 1918 (*L Rogers*)

Lt F W McCarthy. On 9 November, McCarthy was hit in the heel by a spent bullet while ground-strafing. He crashed on landing and was taken to hospital. He was the unit's last casualty of the war (*L Rogers*)

Johnson, Newth and Mackey, who was back from hospital, McCarthy was hit in the heel by a spent bullet. He crashed on returning to base and was sent to hospital, the squadron's last casualty of the war.

Although the war was now all but over, there were still dangers. Stanley J Mason hit an aerial while low flying, his SE 5, having to be replaced, and Lt B S Johnston's machine was hit by anti-aircraft fire at 12,000 feet. With the signing of an armistice imminent, Johnston called enough and ran for home.

On 11 November, the silence of peace fell over the Western Front. Patrols were flown over Mons – where the shooting war had started for the BEF in 1914 – Maubege and Avesnes, but all was strangely quiet in the skies. On 22 November the unit moved for the last time in France, to Inchy, an aerodrome nearly ten miles east of Cambrai. Sports and concerts were organised to pass the time, but the unit was gradually winding down as more and more men were sent to England to be demobilised. On 10 January 1919 all the remaining Canadians left for home. On 22 and 23 January 1919, the last remaining pilots flew the Squadron's aeroplanes to Serny to be ferried to England. On 5 February the unit was reduced to cadre strength: two officers, a WO technical officer, a Sgt Maj and 12 other ranks. This cadre returned to Narborough in England on 17 February 1919 and on New Year's Day 1920 moved again to Bircham Newton, where it was finally disbanded on 22 January.

In its three years of war, No 60 Sqn RFC/RAF had lost 57 aircrew killed in action and another 14 killed or died of injuries in accidents. Nearly 1000 combat reports had been made and over 400 enemy aircraft claimed. It was a proud record.

The aftermath. In June 1919, Frank Soden, an ex-member of No 60 Sqn, was posted to Cologne as part of the occupational forces in Germany. On arrival in the city he found this Nieuport as a trophy at the gates of the aerodrome. The serial number or other markings are unfortunately not visible in the photograph, but Soden's comments in his accompanying letter home indicated that this was Nieuport 17 A6718 of D C G Murray who was taken prisoner on 27 June 1917 (*L Rogers*)

APPENDICES

APPENDIX 1

No 60 SQN COMMANDERS IN FRANCE

Maj Francis F Waldron – 1/5/16 to 3/7/16*

Maj Robert R Smith-Barry – 3/7/16 to 22/12/16

Maj Evelyn P Graves – 22/12/16 to 6/3/17*

Maj Alan John Lance Scott MC – 10/3/17 to 11/7/17**

Maj William John Charles Kennedy Cochran-Patrick DSO
    MC+ – 12/7/17 to 26/12/17

Maj Barry F Moore – 27/12/17 to 12/7/18

Maj James Thomas Byford McCudden VC DSO+MC+ MM –
    Killed in a flying accident while flying to take command.

Maj Cyril Marconi Crowe MC – 13/7/18 to 29/7/18

Maj Alexander C Clarke – 4/8/18 to 4/2/19

* Killed in Action

** Wounded in Action

APPENDIX 2

No 60 SQN AERODROMES

Formed Gosport, England, 1/5/16

To St Omer, France, 25/5/16

To Boisdinghem, France, 31/5/16

To Vert Galant, France, 16/6/16

To St Andre-au-Bois, France, 3/8/16

To Le Hameau, France, 23/8/16

To Savy-Bertlette, France, 1/9/16

To Filescamp Farm, France, 18/1/17

To Ste-Marie-Cappel, France, 7/9/17

To Bailleul, France, 8/3/18

To La Bellevue, France, 23/3/18

To Fienvillers, France, 27/3/18

To Boffles, France, 12/4/18

To Baizieux, France, 17/9/18

To Beugnâtre, France, 13/9/18

To Quiévy, France, 31/10/18

To Inchy, France, 23/11/18

Cadre to Narborough, England, 17/2/19

Cadre to Bircham Newton, England, 1/1/20

Disbanded, Bircham Newton, England, 22/1/20

APPENDIX 3

No 60 SQN WINGS AND BRIGADES

HQ RFC – 25/5/16

HQ 9th Wing – 16/6/16

HQ RFC attached to 13th Wing III Brigade – 3/8/16

Advanced HQ RFC – 23/8/16

13th Wing III Brigade – 1/9/16

11th Wing II Brigade – 7/9/16

13th Wing III Brigade – 23/3/18

APPENDIX 4

No 60 SQN'S TOP-SCORING PILOTS

(Note – Victories scored only while serving with No 60 Sqn)

Capt W A Bishop – 47

Capt A Ball – 31

Capt F O Soden – 16

Capt H A Hamersley – 13

Capt A W Saunders – 13

Capt W J Duncan – 11

Lt W E Jenkins – 11

Capt R L Chidlaw-Roberts – 9

Capt K L Caldwell – 9

Capt J E Doyle – 9

Capt W J Rutherford – 9

Capt G M Duncan – 8

Capt H G Hegarty – 8

Capt W E Molesworth – 8

Capt A D Bell-Irving – 7

Lt J S Griffith – 7

Capt S B Horn – 7

Capt J B Crompton – 6

Capt H Meintjes – 6

Lt S L G Pope – 6

Maj A L Scott – 6

2Lt G C Young – 6

Capt W M Fry – 5

Capt J W Rayner – 5

Lt R K Whitney – 5

APPENDIX 5

No 60 SQN CASUALTIES

Name	Remarks	Date	Aeroplane & Serial
1916			
Maj F Waldron	PoW/DoW	3 July	Morane Bullet A175
Capt N Browning-Paterson	KIA	21 July	Morane Bullet A128
2AM E Deal	WIA	27 July	Morane Biplane A149
Capt L Charles	PoW/DoW	30 July	Morane Biplane A5193
Lt C Williams	KIA	30 July	Morane Biplane A5193
Lt L Whitehead	WIA	30 July	Morane Biplane 5162
Lt W Bryant	WIA	30 July	Morane Biplane 5162
Lt J Ormsby	PoW/DoW	2 August	Morane Biplane 5177
Lt H Newton	DoW	2 August	Morane Biplane 5177
Sgt A Walker	KIA	2 August	Morane Biplane 5181
2Lt L Clark	KIA	2 August	Morane Biplane 5181
2Lt J Drysdale	WIA	25 August	Nieuport 16 A187
2Lt B Wainwright	PoW	28 August	Morane Bullet A173
Capt F Goodrich	DOI	12 September	Morane Bullet A166
Capt A Summers	KIA	15 September	Nieuport 16 A136
Capt H Tower	KIA	19 September	Morane Bullet A204
Lt G Phillipi	WIA	26 September	Nieuport 16 5172
2Lt C King	KIFA	30 September	Nieuport 17 A201
Lt N McL Robertson	KIFA	17 October	Morane Bullet A219
2Lt W Carlyle	KIA	26 October	Nieuport 16 A133
Lt M Spenser	KIA	3 November	Nieuport 16 A125
Capt A Bell-Irving	WIA	9 November	Nieuport 17 A272
2Lt H Martin	KIFA	16 November	Nieuport 16 A135
Lt D Bacon	KIA	16 November	Nieuport 16 A225
Capt G Parker	KIA	27 November	Nieuport 17 A281
Capt E Grenfell	WIA	11 December	Nieuport 17 A278
Capt E Gilchrist	IIA	11 December	Nieuport 17 A276
1917			
2Lt R Hopper	KIFA	1 January	Nieuport 16 A187
2Lt E Herbert	WIA	28 January	Artillery duty
2Lt B Roxburgh-Smith	IIA	24 February	Nieuport 16 A164
Lt P Joyce	KIA	6 March	Nieuport 16 A208
Maj E Graves	KIA	6 March	Nieuport 17 A213
Lt A Whitehead	WIA/PoW	11 March	Nieuport 17 A279
2Lt H Brackenbury	IIA	23 March	Nieuport 16 A224
Lt C Caffyn	KIA	28 March	Nieuport 17 A6673
Lt W Garnett	KIA	30 March	Nieuport 17 A273
2Lt F Bower	DoW	30 March	Nieuport 23 A6774
2Lt V Williams	KIA	2 April	Nieuport 17 A6763
Lt E Townesend	WIA/PoW	5 April	Nieuport 17 A6693
2Lt C Hall	KIA	7 April	Nieuport 23 A 6766
2Lt G Smart	KIA	7 April	Nieuport 17 A6645
2 Lt D Robertson	WIA	7 April	Nieuport 17 A311
Capt M Knowles	PoW	7 April	Nieuport 17 A6773

Name	Remarks	Date	Aeroplane & Serial
Maj J Milot	KIA	8 April	Nieuport 23 A6764
2Lt H Hervey	PoW	8 April	Nieuport 17 A311
Lt W Russell	PoW	14 April	Nieuport 17 A6796
2Lt L Chapman	PoW	14 April	Nieuport 23 B1523
2Lt J Cock	KIA	14 April	Nieuport 23 B1511
Capt A Binnie	WIA/PoW	14 April	Nieuport 23 A6772
Lt J McC Elliot	KIA	16 April	Nieuport 23 B1509
2Lt R Kimbell	KIA	16 April	Nieuport 23 A6769
2Lt D Robertson	KIA	16 April	Nieuport 23 B1501
2Lt T Langwill	PoW	16 April	Nieuport 23 B1507
Lt F Atkinson	IIA	20 April	Nieuport 17 B1513
2Lt R Clark	DoW	24 April	Nieuport 23 A6777
2Lt N Henderson	IIA	26 April	Nieuport 23 B1549
2Lt F Stedman	Lost FTL/PoW	27 April	Nieuport 23 B1570
2Lt H Ross	IIA	28 April	Nieuport 23 B1512
2Lt C McKissock	PoW	6 May	Nieuport 23 B1514
Lt G Hunter	WIA/PoW	6 May	Nieuport 23 B1597
2Lt R Grandin	KIA	18 May	Nieuport 23 A6770
2Lt W Gilchrist	WIA/PoW	25 May	Nieuport 23 A6776
2Lt R Phalen	KIA	28 May	Nieuport 23 B1624
Lt C Blake	IIA	30 May	Nieuport 23 B1576
2Lt R Harris	KIFA	7 June	Nieuport 17 B1503
Lt D Lloyd	KIA	16 June	Nieuport 23 B1610
Lt D Murray	WIA/PoW	27 June	Nieuport 17 A6718
Lt A Adam	WIA/PoW/DoW	3 July	Nieuport 23 B1585
Maj A Scott	WIA	10 July	Nieuport 23 B1575
2Lt G Parkes	WIA/PoW	15 July	Nieuport 23 B1575
Lt W Gunner	KIA	29 July	SE 5 A8937
2Lt M West-Thompson	IIA	19 August	SE 5 A8930
2Lt H Hammond	PoW	14 September	SE 5 A8918
2Lt J Hawtrey	PoW/DoW	16 September	SE 5 A8909
Sgt J Bancroft	PoW	20 September	SE 5a A8931
Capt K Law	KIA	21 September	SE 5 A8914
Lt J Whiting	KIA	22 September	SE 5a B4864
Lt I MacGregor	WIA	22 September	SE 5a B4860
2AM H Bright	KIA	23 September	SE 5a B557
2Lt I Lawrence	IIFA	24 September	SE 5a B550
2Lt J Flynn	KIFA	30 September	SE 5a B522
2Lt J Fitzgerald	PoW	5 October	SE 5a B507
Lt W Sherwood	KIA	27 October	SE 5a B534
Capt J Caunter	KIA	28 October	SE 5a B4873
Capt C Temperley	WIA	28 October	SE 5a B565
Lt S Pope	WIA	18 November	SE 5a B519
2Lt W Jenkins	KIFA	23 November	SE 5a B608
2Lt M West-Thompson	KIFA	23 November	SE 5a B553
2Lt R Maclennan	DOI	23 December	SE 5a B6

1918

Capt F Selous	KIA	4 January	SE 5a C5334
Lt A Morey	KIA	24 January	SE 5a B4897

Name	Remarks	Date	Aeroplane & Serial
2Lt C Ball	PoW	5 February	SE 5a B533
2Lt N Royston	IIA	18 February	SE 5a C9487
Lt G Craig	PoW/DoW	21 February	SE 5a C5325
Lt W Kent	KIA	21 February	SE 5a B4860
2Lt J Louw	IIA	4 March	SE 5a B625
Lt L Southwell	IIA	6 March	SE 5a C5343
	DOI	14 March	
Capt H Crompton	IIA	15 March	SE 5a B545
2Lt E Christie	KIA	2 April	SE 5a B8326
Capt K Crawford	KIA	11 April	SE 5a C5445
Lt H Proctor	KIA	16 May	SE 5a D3912
Lt J Hadham	KIFA	30 May	SE 5a C5381
2Lt G Duncan	IIA	9 June	SE 5a B8398
Capt J Belgrave	KIA	13 June	SE 5a D5988
Lt R Lewis	PoW	13 June	SE 5a C9498
Lt K Campbell	IIA	27 June	SE 5a C8858
Lt F Read USAS	WIA	2 July	SE 5a B151
Lt H Gordon	KIA	7 July	SE 5a B137
Maj J McCudden	KIFA	9 July	SE 5a C1126
Capt G Dell-Clarke	KIFA	16 July	SE 5a D5992
Lt G du Cros	IIFA	17 July	SE 5a E1306
2Lt J Griffith	FTL INJ	18 July	SE 5a D3503
Lt J MacVicker	KIA	22 July	SE 5a D6183
Lt L Loughran USAS	KIFA	28 July	SE 5a E1261
Capt C Parry	IIFA	29 July	SE 5a D360
Capt O Scholte	IIRoad acc	29 July	
	DOI	30 July	
2Lt J Hall	KIA	8 August	SE 5a B151
2Lt H Buckley	WIA	10 August	SE 5a C6662
2Lt R Whitney	WIA	11 August	SE 5a C8886
Lt J Anderson	KIA	13 August	SE 5a D6979
Lt E McCracken	PoW	13 August	SE 5a E1308
Lt S Keen	DoW	21 August	SE 5a C1131
2Lt 2Lt S Thomson	KIA	5 September	SE 5a C1876
Lt R Blessley USAS	WIA	5 September	SE 5a E4070
Capt J Doyle	WIA/PoW	5 September	SE5a E1397
2Lt H Stuart-Smith	KIA	15 September	SE 5a D6981
Lt J Smith	KIA	17 September	SE 5a C9297
2Lt H Battle	WIA	20 September	SE 5a D6945
Lt G Caswell	WIA	20 September	SE 5a F5472
Lt L H Smith	PoW	25 September	SE 5a E1276
2Lt L Stockwell	PoW	28 October	SE 5a H690
Lt N Mackay	IIFA	1 November	SE 5a E1390
Lt F Osborne	IIFA	3 November	SE 5a F910
Lt F McCarthy	WIA	9 November	SE 5a E6007

Key

KIA – Killed in action	WIA – Wounded in action	PoW – Prisoner of war
DoW – Died of wounds	DOI – Died of injuries	IIA – Injured in accident
IIFA – Injured in flying accident	KIFA – Killed in flying accident	FTL – Forced to land

COLOUR PLATES

1

Morane-Saulnier Type BB 5182 of Capt A S M Summers, Vert Galant, France, June 1916

This Morane was issued to No 60 Sqn on 31 May 1916. It was flown by Capts Tower and Summers until wrecked in a landing crash in August and struck off strength.

2

Morane-Saulnier Type BB 5181 of Sgt A Walker, St-André-au Bois, France, August 1916

Issued to the unit in May 1916, this Morane was shot down by anti-aircraft fire on 2 August 1916. The pilot, Sgt A Walker and his observer, 2Lt L L Clark, were both killed.

3

Morane-Saulnier Type LA A143 of 2Lt C A Ridley, St-André-au Bois, France, August 1916

This Parasol LA was issued to No 60 Sqn for the express purpose of landing spies behind the German lines. Flown by 2Lt C A Ridley on such a mission, it was forced to land in enemy territory by engine trouble and was destroyed by Ridley.

4

Morane-Saulnier Type N A122 of Capt R R Smith-Barry, Vert Galant, France, June 1916

This Bullet was issued to the unit on 30 May 1916 and flown by Capt Smith-Barry. On 3 June it force landed due to engine failure, damaged and struck off strength.

5

Morane-Saulnier Type N A173 of 2Lt B M Wainwright, Le Hameau, France, August 1916

This machine was issued twice to No 60 Sqn. After being damaged in a forced landing on 21 June 1916 it was re-issued on 8 August. Flown by several pilots, it was finally shot down on 28 August 1916, the pilot, 2Lt B M Wainwright, taken prisoner.

6

Morane-Saulnier Type I A199 of 2Lt H Meintjes, Le Hameau, France, September 1916

Issued on 22 July 1916, this 110 hp Bullet was flown by R Smith-Barry and H Meintjes, but more often by 2Lt W M Fry, who flew it from 4 October to 18 October when it was returned to 2AD.

7

Morane-Saulnier Type V A204 of Capt H C Tower, Savy, France, September 1916

This Bullet was issued to the unit on 12 August 1916 and flown by 2Lt D V Armstrong. On 19 September it was lost in action, its pilot, Capt H C Tower, was killed.

8

Nieuport 16 A135 of Lt P E M Le Gallais, Savy, France, October 1916

This Nieuport was flown first by the RNAS. It was sent to 1ASD on 24 April 1916. It served in No 1 Sqn from 7 August until 18 August when it was transferred to No 60 Sqn. Shown here equipped with Le Prieur rockets, it was flown by Lt J D Latta who was credited with five

victories, including two balloons. It was finally wrecked in a landing crash by 2Lt H E Martin, who was killed.

9

Nieuport 16 A125 of Lt J M J Spenser, Savy, France, November 1916

First issued to No 1 Sqn this Nieuport was issued to No 60 Sqn on 28 September 1916. It was lost in action on 3 November 1916. Its pilot, Lt J M J Spenser, was taken prisoner but later died of his wounds.

10

Nieuport 17 A201 of Capt A Ball, Savy, France, August 1916

Capt Ball brought this Nieuport with him as his personal machine when he was posted from No 11 Sqn to No 60 Sqn on 23 August 1916. While with No 60 Sqn Ball flew mainly Nieuports A201 and A213, scoring six victories while flying the former and 11 victories flying A213. One, or possibly both, were fitted with a *cone de penetration*, painted red. No photographs of either aeroplane in Ball's Flight markings are known to exist and the Flight markings shown are speculative.

11

Nieuport 17 A274 of 2Lt W M Fry, Filescamp Farm, France, February 1917

This Nieuport was inherited by 2Lt William M Fry from his Flight commander, Capt Henry 'Duke' Meintjes. Meintjes had scored two victories while flying A274 and Fry shared an Albatros C type and an Albatros D type forced to land. A274 was finally blown over in landing by Lt W P Garnett on 24 March 1917 and dismantled for spares.

12

Nieuport 17 A6646 of 2Lt K L Caldwell, Filescamp Farm, France, February 1917

This Nieuport was collected from 2ASD by Lt Keith Caldwell on 28 January 1917, reporting that it was 'very nose heavy'. Fitted with a camera, it was flown by Caldwell on photographic and escort missions in addition to his normal offensive patrols, until he departed on leave on 6 March. It was damaged in a forced landing on 24 March and struck off strength.

13

Nieuport 17 A311 of 2Lt H E Hervey, Filescamp Farm, France, April 1917

This Nieuport was issued to the unit on 14 December 1916. First flown by Meintjes who scored two victories while flying it on 29 January 1917, it was lost in action on 8 April 1917 when 2Lt H E Hervey was shot down by anti-aircraft fire and taken prisoner.

14

Nieuport 23 B1514 2Lt C W McKissock, Filescamp Farm, France, May 1917

This machine was delivered to the unit from 1ASD by Lt C Patteson on 8 April 1917. It was lost in action on 6 May 1917 when its pilot, 2Lt C W McKissock, was forced to land and taken prisoner.

15
Nieuport 23 B1514 in German hands, Cambrai, France, May 1917

McKissock's B1514 was over-painted in German markings by Offstv Paul Baeumer of *Fl Abt* 7 who flew it in several operational flights. Baeumer later became a noted fighter pilot, surviving the war with 43 victories.

16
Nieuport 23 B1597 of 2Lt G D Hunter, Filescamp Farm, France, May 1917

Lt W Fry collected this Nieuport from 2ASD on 28 April 1917. Fry scored two victories while flying this Nieuport, but it was lost on 6 May 1917 when 2Lt G D Hunter was wounded, forced to land and taken prisoner.

17
Nieuport 23 B1575 of Maj A J L Scott, Filescamp Farm, France, June 1917

This Nieuport was collected from 2ASD on 17 April by Lt W A Bishop. It was flown by Maj A J L Scott, who shot down an Albatros DIII on 2 May. It was damaged in combat on 28 May, but Scott was unhurt and scored a further victory – an Albatros DIII in flames – while flying it on 10 July. On 15 July, it was lost in action. Its pilot, Lt G A H Parkes, was wounded and taken prisoner.

18
Nieuport 17 A6718 of Lt D C G Murray, Filescamp Farm, France, June 1917

Issued to No 60 Sqn on 22 March 1917, this machine suffered a wing failure on 30 April. Repaired, it was lost on 26 June when Lt D C G Murray was wounded and taken prisoner.

19
Nieuport 23 B1566 of Lt W A Bishop, Filescamp Farm, France, July 1917

Perhaps the most famous Nieuport in the RFC, B1566 was flown by Lt/Capt W A Bishop who claimed 29 victories in this machine. It was later issued to No 1 Sqn and wrecked on 17 August 1917. After repair it was sent to Egypt in a packing case on 2 November 1917, allocated to X Flight on 10 April 1918 and flown to Aqaba on 28 September 1918, where it was dismantled, repacked and sent to 19 TDS at El Rimal on 5 November 1918.

20
SE 5 A4853 of Capt F O Soden, Filescamp Farm, France, August 1917

This SE 5 was one of the first production batch of 24 SE 5s. Previously issued to No 56 Sqn and flown by Lt C A Lewis, it was issued to No 60 Sqn on 12 August 1917. It was flown by Capt F O Soden, but was returned to 2ASD on 21 August, possibly to be re-engined.

21
SE 5 A8936 of Capt W A Bishop, Filescamp Farm, France, August 1917

Issued to the unit on 20 July 1917, A8936 was flown by Capt W A Bishop who claimed 11 victories in this SE 5. It was later flown by Lts S B Horn, Whiting and West-Thompson. It was finally struck off strength on 20 September 1917.

22
SE 5a A8898 of Capt K L Caldwell, Filescamp Farm, France, September 1917

After use by No 56 Sqn, this SE 5 was sent to the depot and re-engined as a 200 hp SE5a and reissued to No 56 Sqn on 15 June 1917. Issued to No 60 Sqn on 20 August, it was flown by Capt K L Caldwell until he was posted to Home Establishment in October 1917.

23
SE 5 A8932 of Capt W E Molesworth, Filescamp Farm, France, September 1917

This SE 5 was issued to No 60 Sqn on 5 August 1917. It was first flown by Capt W E Molesworth, who scored one victory while flying it, and then by Capt R L Chidlaw-Roberts, who scored four of his total of ten victories in this SE 5.

24
SE 5a A8918 of Lt H T Hammond, Ste-Marie-Cappel, France, September 1917

Previously issued to No 56 Sqn, this SE 5 was returned to 2ASD on 15 August 1917. It was issued to No 60 Sqn, possibly re-engined as a 200 hp SE 5a, on 21 August. It was damaged and forced to land by ground fire on 14 September 1917. The pilot, Lt H T Hammond, was taken prisoner.

25
SE 5a B507 of 2Lt J J Fitzgerald, Ste-Marie-Cappel, France, October 1917

Another ex-No 56 Sqn SE 5a, this machine was issued to No 60 Sqn on 10 September 1917. On 5 October 1917, 2Lt J J Fitzgerald was forced to land at Harlebeke, the base of *Jasta* 18, by engine failure and was taken prisoner.

26
SE 5a D6945 of Capt A Beck, Boffles, France, August 1918

This SE 5a was issued to the unit on 28 July 1918. It is shown here while being flown by Capt A Beck who claimed four victories in this machine.

27
SE 5a D6953 of Capt J W Rayner, Baizieux, France, October 1918

Issued to the unit on 24 August 1918, this SE5a was flown by Capt J W Rayner, the A Flight commander, from 28 August until 25 October 1918. Rayner claimed all five of his victories while flying this machine.

28
SE 5a F5687 of Lt USAS J A Roth, Quièvy, France, November 1918

One of the last SE 5as issued to No 60 Sqn, this was a presentation aeroplane 'Sallie Parker' donated by Mr H P Stromberg of New York City. Appropriately, it was flown by a fellow countryman, Lt USAS J A Roth, and is shown here in B Flight markings.

GLOSSARY OF GERMAN TERMS

Fl Abt. Flieger Abteilung – Aviation unit. Field Flying section for reconnaissance and photography

Fl Abt (A). Flieger Abteilung – Aviation unit co-operating with artillery

Jagdgeschwader. JG – Group of four *Jagdstaffeln* (approx. 50 aeroplanes)

Jagdstaffel. Jasta – Fighter unit

Jagdstaffeln. – Fighter units

Kasta. Kampfstaffel. – Fighting section

Kraftwagenflak. K-Flak – Mobile anti-aircraft gun

Luftstreitkräfte. – Air force

Schlachtstaffel. Schlasta – The *Schutzstaffeln* were renamed *Schlachtstaffel* in March 1918

Schutzstaffel. Schusta – Unit of two-seater aeroplanes for the protection of *Flieger Abteilung* and *Flieger Abteilung (A)* aeroplanes

BIBLIOGRAPHY AND SOURCES

FRY, WG CDR W M, *Air of Battle*, William Kimber, London, 1974

HARVEY, H E, *Cage Birds*, Penguin, London, 1940

HENSHAW, T, *The Sky Their Battlefield*, Grub St, London, 1995

O'CONNOR, M AND DAVIS, M, *Nieuports in RNAS RFC and RAF Service*, Cross & Cockade International, 2007

SCOTT, A J L, *Sixty Squadron*, Heinemann, London, 1920

WARNE, JOE, '*60 Squadron* – A detailed history', Cross & Cockade International Vol 11 Nos 1 to 4 and Vol 12 No 1

Popular Flying, various issues, 1930s

Log books of K L Caldwell and W M Fry

INDEX

References to illustrations are shown in **bold**. Plates are shown with page and caption locators in brackets.